MIND,
BRAIN,
BODY

MIND, BRAIN, BODY

Toward a Convergence of

Psychoanalysis and Neurobiology

MORTON F. REISER

Basic Books, Inc., Publishers   *New York*

Excerpt from Sigmund Freud, "Inhibitions, Symptoms and Anxiety" (1926) in *The Standard Edition of the Complete Psychological Works of Sigmund Freud,* trans. and edited by James Strachey, vol. 20 (London: Hogarth Press, 1959), pp. 134–40. Reprinted by permission of Sigmund Freud Copyrights Ltd., The Institute of Psycho-Analysis, and the Hogarth Press Ltd.

Excerpt from E. R. Kandel, *A Cell Biological Approach to Learning* (Bethesda, Md.: Society for Neuroscience, 1978), pp. 4–5. Reprinted by permission of the author and the Society for Neuroscience.

Excerpts from "Converging Sectors of Psychoanalysis and Neurobiology: Mutual Challenge and Opportunities," Presidential Address, The American Psychoanalytic Association, December 1983, by Morton F. Reiser, M.D. With permission of The American Psychoanalytic Association and International Universities Press, publisher of the *Journal of the American Psychoanalytic Association.*

Excerpt reprinted by permission of the publisher from "Implications of a Biopsychosocial Model for Research in Psychiatry" by M. F. Reiser, *Psychosomatic Medicine* 42, no. 1:11 (Supplement 1980). Copyright 1980 by The American Psychosomatic Society, Inc.

Library of Congress Cataloging in Publication Data

Reiser, Morton F.
  Mind, brain, body.

  Bibliography: p. 215
  Includes index
  1. Mental illness—Physiological aspects.
2. Mind and body. 3. Psychoanalysis. 4. Neurobiology.
5. Stress (Psychology) 6. Stress (Physiology) I. Title.
RC455.4.B5R45 1984   616.89'07   83-46069
ISBN 0-465-04603-7

For Lynn

In countless and untold ways,

knowing ponds and angler,

she supported, cajoled, encouraged and

helped find places and times

when the trout were rising.

CONTENTS

Part III

BRAIN

THE NEUROBIOLOGIC SIDE

Part IV

BODY

IMPLICATIONS FOR CLINICAL MEDICINE AND PSYCHIATRY

ACKNOWLEDGMENTS

THERE ARE so many people to thank. Some, responding to my request, gave direct counsel and advice. Others, without knowing—long before I had ever thought of writing this or any other book—contributed indirectly through their critical formative influences as teachers and mentors; still others, also unknowingly, through collaboration in common tasks and through exchanges of ideas in formal and informal conversations.

Preliminary drafts of various chapters were reviewed and commented on by Floyd Bloom, Michael Davis, Marshall Edelson, Stephen Fleck, Patricia Goldman-Rakic, George Heninger, Eric Kandel, Hans Loewald, Mortimer Mishkin, Eugene Redmond, and Lynn Whisnant Reiser. I am also indebted to the many colleagues who offered valuable comments and questions in response to presentations of earlier versions of some of the material at various psychiatric and psychoanalytic society meetings and seminars during the past few years.

Many of the ideas developed in this book represent germinations of stimuli first encountered in exposures to early teachers and exemplars, especially I. Arthur Mirsky, David McKenzie Rioch, Saul Korey, Milton Rosenbaum, Otto Isakower, Edith Jacobson, Charles Fisher, Seymour Lustman, and Robert Waelder.

Later I learned and profited immeasurably from collaborations and extensive discussions with Herbert Weiner and with

Margaret Thaler Singer, and from briefer but critically important conversations with Myron Hofer.

The opportunity to serve on various study sections of the National Institute of Mental Health, particularly the Board of Scientific Counselors of the Intramural Research Program, and on the Committee on Research and Special Training of the American Psychoanalytic Association provided me with continuing exposure to new data and developments in research. I am indeed indebted to the many colleagues with whom I shared these experiences and from whom I learned so much.

Three persons, already mentioned, warrant further note. Marshall Edelson has taught me much that has been of great help in sharpening, extending, and developing ideas. Discussions with him have also been personally supportive and encouraging in important ways. Lynn Whisnant Reiser, in addition to giving support and encouragement, has contributed throughout and to all phases of the work, including development of the text. I owe special thanks to Eric Kandel. His research and publications did much to inspire this effort, and his personal support provided the extra courage I needed to take up the challenge.

I am indebted to Harriette Borsuch, who helped prepare the manuscript, and to Judy Guy, who has patiently and with editorial skill typed and typed and retyped, and helped to organize innumerable drafts.

Thanks for permission to include excerpts from previous writings are due to Eric Kandel, Hoyle Leigh, Smith Kline & French Laboratories, the Society for Neuroscience, *Psychosomatic Medicine, Journal of Psychosomatic Research,* Basic Books, Hogarth Press, and International Universities Press, Inc., publishers of *The Journal of the American Psychoanalytic Association.*

Finally I want to acknowledge the special editorial wisdom and skill of Jo Ann Miller of Basic Books, and to thank her for guidance and help in bringing the book to completion.

MIND,
BRAIN,
BODY

Introduction

THIS BOOK is written in response to a challenge: Do psycho-analysis and neurobiology—each with a great deal to say about mental processes—have anything to say to each other? Indeed, this question poses an interesting rhetorical paradox with far-reaching theoretical implications. But it can also be understood to be part of—indeed, partly to have arisen from— the everyday empirical context of clinical practice.

Medicine encompasses a vast range of disciplines, from the preclinical (life) sciences—relatively graceful, elegant, and sat-isfying in method and theory—to the clinical disciplines—sci-ence and art, relatively stolid and steady. Although clinical work is becoming more precise, it is often still clumsy, groping, and frustrating. And clinical practice is always pragmatic, obliged to be humanistic as it deals with the pain and discom-fort arising from physical and mental frailties of the human organism.

In all branches of medicine, the sheer pace and volume of progress in the basic sciences have overshadowed and overpowered work in the clinical arena. Students and clinicians alike turn increasingly to reductionistic science, understandably hoping that it will ultimately render clinical science more effective and clinical art unnecessary. Nowhere is this more true than in psychiatry. For a time, after World War II, psychoanalysis was regarded as holding promise not only of advancing our understanding of mental illness, including etiology and pathogenesis, but also of providing a scientific psychological basis for the clinical art of nonpsychiatric medical practice, as well as of psychiatry itself. Progress during the past thirty years in the neurosciences, especially neurobiology, is now overshadowing clinical psychodynamic considerations in the clinical arena. Advances in neuropsychopharmacology have made possible revolutionary changes in the management of major psychiatric disorders including affective disorders and the psychoses. While the psychopharmacologic agents do not cure the basic underlying diseases, they alter the function of critically important brain systems in ways that control symptoms and alter the clinical course of those diseases. They permit earlier recovery, briefer hospital treatment, and earlier return of patients to their families and communities. Patients can then be maintained on drug regimens—optimally in combination with psychological and psychosocial treatment modalities. Despite some of the problems—communities have not always been adequately prepared to receive patients, and some of the drugs produce serious disabling side effects, such as tardive dyskinesia—the net clinical gain is nothing short of miraculous.

But advances in clinical psychopharmacology represent only one small part of the total picture—of the many interrelated technological and conceptual breakthroughs along the entire advancing frontier of neuroscience. In animal studies, drugs used along with recently developed arrays of techniques and methods that permit anatomic, neuropsychologic, neurophysiologic, neurochemical, neuropharmacologic, cell biologic, molecular biologic, molecular genetic, and developmental analyses have demonstrated in detail a myriad of brain mechanisms that subserve behavior and higher mental functions in health and in disease. Does this mean, as some assert, that in the long run full explanations of mental events will be provided by neurobiology and chemicals will replace psychology in the clinic? An affirmative conclusion would imply that it would be reasonable ultimately to expect unified understanding of brain and mind in the same terms. I, as well as many others, do not think so. It is, I think, fair to say that the pendulum has swung too far and to say it without diminishing by one whit the importance and significance of the advances in the realm of neurobiology.

The Mind-Brain Interface

As Edelson (1984) has pointed out, *mental and biological phenomena occupy different domains.* Qualitative and quantitative characteristics of composite units within each of the two realms can only be studied independently of each other and by different methods, and composite units belonging to different realms can be described only in different terms. Descriptions are not interchangeable between the two domains, and concepts belonging to one cannot be directly articulated with concepts belonging to the other.[1]

At least for the present we confront an interface between mind and brain-body that is best approached with the explicit recognition that the realm of mind, which deals with meanings, and the realm of brain-body,* which deals with matter and energy, are separated by a composite series of semantic, conceptual, and methodological discontinuities. The science of the mind and the science of the brain-body use different languages,

---

*In confronting the interface between mind and brain I regard mind as belonging to the realm of meaning; brain and body to the realm of matter and energy—hence the use of the hyphenated expression "brain-body" in this context.

different methods, and different concepts organized at different levels of abstraction. From the fact of these differences there follow several corollaries:

1. What we wish to know but do not know is how nonphysical stimuli (meanings, symbols) are transduced into physical physiological events somewhere in the brain-body (Weiner 1972); or in the opposite direction, how physiological brain events in brain-body are transduced into meanings.
2. As Steven Rose (1978) has pointed out, a phenomenon connected with human experience, such as anger, is capable of valid and complete description in either mind language or brain language, but *confusion and mistakes inevitably result from trying to locate causes at one level to consequences at the other.*
3. Consequently, there are frustrating limits to the depth of understanding that can be achieved by demonstrating that correlations exist between events that can be concomitantly recorded by the separate methods and described by the separate languages of two realms—no matter how precise and sophisticated the methods and descriptions may be. Combined physiological-psychological studies of sleep and dreaming are outstanding examples of the coexistent methodological powers and explanatory limitations inherent in this approach.

This book responds to these challenges first, by identifying, from selected sectors of psychoanalysis and neurobiology, data that pertain to common problems such as memory and anxiety; second, by attempting to discern patterns or principles in the independently derived sets of data, suggesting that the data may indeed be converging; and third, by working toward an empirical clinical perspective on some of the important but unanswered questions generated along the way.

This task will not be without its difficulties for writer and reader alike. Although, as I hope to make clear in the opening chapters, psychoanalysis and neurobiology could and should relate in complementary, mutually enriching—rather than mutually exclusive or unrelated—ways, there are at present difficulties, major difficulties, in relating the disciplines. While neurobiology, a natural science, has been growing and advancing rapidly in ways already described, some aspects of developments in psychoanalysis have carried it in directions that lead away from the natural sciences.

For example, metapsychological theory, while useful, perhaps even necessary for certain purposes, has led psychoanalysis into a virtual *cul de sac* that is isolated from empirical and conceptual articulation with biological sciences. When theoretical constructs that are beyond the reach of psychological and physical methods are regarded as *real,* the possibilities for fruitful dialogue and conceptual articulation with the natural sciences slip away.[2] But there are clinical psychological data —"raw" process data—that are accessible and psychological theorems based upon them that are open to empirical validation within the realm of psychoanalytic psychology itself. And these raw clinical data even have the potential to generate questions that ultimately could be productively addressed by neurobiologic methods in neurobiologic model systems and preparations.

The approach to be developed in this book is basically empirical. It involves first studying data from each realm—mind and brain-body—separately and then tracking the data from the two in parallel—a dual-track approach. As will be apparent in the text, the methodological asymmetry between the two realms is immense, and the data from each of them ask for a different mind-set in reading. On each side—mental and biological—I have presented data selected for the task at hand and have attempted to include sufficient detail to permit the reader to make a firsthand appraisal not only of the findings, but also of the method, the logic, and style, if you will, of the investigative endeavor. Direct "raw data" from the clinical psychoanalytic process (e.g., pertaining to complex memory systems as manifest in dreams and free associations) will supply the findings from the mental realm. The data from the neurobiologic realm will come from experimental laboratory studies of actual structures and actual physiologic events involved in the realm of brain function (e.g., transsynaptic neurotransmitter mechanisms and cell biology of neurons in simple animals undergoing primitive forms of learning).

The Plan of the Book

In its sequential plan, the book uses the stress response paradigm as an implicit organizing theme. The nature of the challenge is developed in part I. Part II, "Mind," deals with the mental realm, with the cognitive processes involved in recognition and evaluation of internal and external sources of danger. Part III, "Brain," deals with the biological realm, with the cortical and subcortical brain systems involved in recognition and evaluation of internal and external sources of danger and in the activation of the stress response systems. It is the challenge of trying to understand what occurs in the interface between the mental and biological realms, as they are simultaneously involved in cognitive processes and in activating stress response systems (transduction of meanings into physiologic events) that is the most difficult. There is little historical precedent and a paucity of reliable guidelines for attempting such an understanding. We can illustrate the serious gap in our knowledge at this interface. For example, picture the following scenario: It is Sunday afternoon during the football season, and hundreds of thousands of people across the nation are watching a television broadcast of an important championship game. With the score tied, in the closing play, a long pass thrown deep into the end zone is intercepted and run all the way back down the field—scoring the winning touchdown for the team that intercepted. Three middle-aged men watching this rousing finish may drop dead from cardiac arrest. Now, and here is the point, if the pass had not been intercepted but had been caught by a player from the passing team (scoring the winning touchdown for that team), three other middle-aged men would be the ones likely to suffer cardiac arrest. So somehow the meaning —something without physical properties—determines the occurrence of actual electrophysiologic events in the victims' brains and then hearts. For either finish, the physical stimuli and the television display would, of course, be the same for all viewers. But who the victims are would depend on which team won. We know how the nervous system transduces acoustic

vibrations (one form of physical energy) into electrophysiologic impulses (another form of physical energy). But we do
not know how the nervous system works when stimuli are
transduced from the nonphysical realm of meaning to the physical realm of physiology, as in the football example, or in the
case of auditory signals, from physical electrophysiologic impulses to the cognate meaning of spoken words.

The dual-track approach will carry us to the edge of the gap
from each side and then search for hints of bridging principles,
seeking an empirical perspective for psychoanalysis. Then,
having finessed rather than solved the issues presented by the
gap, the text moves into clearer and more familiar territory, an
area of great importance for clinical psychiatry and medicine
—namely, the neurobiology of stress response systems and the
psychophysiology of stress (including autonomic, psychoneuroendocrine, and psychoneuroimmune response systems). It is at
this juncture that physiologic data pertaining to the centrally
important issue of transduction are reviewed at length. This
discussion bridges naturally to part IV, "Body," which surveys
the clinical sequelae of stress in peripheral tissues and organs
("psychosomatic medicine") and in brain (psychiatric disorders). Here an overall model is developed which proposes that
major functional psychoses represent "stress diseases" in
which the brain is the target organ. Finally, there is further
speculation—"Toward a Theory."

The book is addressed to clinicians, neuroscientists, psychiatric residents, students, and any others who are interested in
understanding the nature of the human species and the lives
and behavior of individual men and women. Naturally, each
reader will be more interested in and conversant with one
realm or the other. In presenting each side I have attempted to
supply those on one side with enough detail for them to find the
account credible, convincing, and even stimulating without
"losing" those on the other by confronting them with material
that may seem too detailed, obscure, or strange. I have assumed that most readers will want to follow both sides, and I
hope I have succeeded in rendering each sufficiently accessible
("reader friendly"). The sections where the material is unfamil-

9

iar and even seems too detailed may be the very ones in which the persistent reader will find interesting and worthwhile new information and ideas. Readers with primary backgrounds in biology who prefer to embark from more familiar ground may choose to address part III ("Brain") before taking on part II ("Mind"). The material in each part is presented so as to make this reordering feasible (though less desirable for following the thematic argument).

This is a book I had to write. The challenge has intrigued me continuously ever since I moved some forty years ago from the fascinating studies of the preclinical years to the fascinating challenge of the clinic. While too many of my colleagues ask if I still really take psychoanalysis seriously, too many others ask an opposite question—why am I still interested in neurobiology? The pages that follow are an attempt to give one answer to both questions.

NOTES

1. It is conceivable that units in each realm could progressively be further subdivided and reduced into subunits that would ultimately be the same, but in this case these ultimate units would be part of a different (an inorganic) realm that would be neither mental nor biological. Rather, this third realm would be basic to the higher order (mental and biological) emergent phenomena encountered in each of the other two realms. For example, this third realm could perhaps turn out to be small particle physics. But that is a statement of faith—a reductionistic "credo." Such a reduction may or may not be capable of realization—but certainly not, as the saying goes, in our lifetimes.

2. It should be added here that psychoanalysis shares interests not only with the natural sciences, but also with a wide variety of behavioral and social sciences, as well as with many of the humanities, linguistics, religion, jurisprudence, and numerous other disciplines.

In focusing on the interface between psychoanalysis and neurobiology, I do not mean to imply that these other interfaces are not important. What is important will depend on context. For example, mind-body issues are not the most important or relevant ones for understanding and illuminating transactions involved in the clinical conduct of psychoanalysis—in that context, issues of language, meaning, and motive have more immediate relevance and technical utility.

Part I

TOWARD AN EMPIRICAL APPROACH

CHAPTER 1

The Challenge–A Gap Between the Mental and Biological Realms

GOOD QUESTIONS, like bad pennies, have a way of turning up over and over again. So it is with dilemmas belonging to the still obscure and mysterious nature of relationships between mind and brain, brain and body. At first glance, if one depends upon everyday experience and common sense, there might seem to be no problem at all. The brain is part of the body, it regulates and is regulated by all the rest of the body, and clearly it is the organ that subserves the collection of functions we call mind. Further, it is well known that states of mind can affect the body in profound ways. Problems of living, emotional stresses, and a wide variety of conflictual life situations and events are known to be frequent antecedents of illness—sometimes even of sudden death. On the other hand, efficient psychological function and emotional stability are conducive to, and supportive of, bodily health. So—what are the questions? Why use terms like "mysterious" and "obscure"?

The questions begin and will, I suppose, end with wondering how the human organism really works. An inquisitive youngster tries to break open a watch to see how it works, how it comes about that when you wind it, it ticks and keeps time. The same or another inquiring mind knows that when you drop an apple, it falls to the ground, but wonders why and how that happens. Albert Einstein, who uncovered more about such questions than any physicist before him, was unable to give a finite answer to them. He compared our quest for understanding how the universe operates—for understanding its ultimate nature—to wanting to see into the inner workings of a watch that is forever locked (Einstein 1938). Since we cannot open the watch and look inside, we can only surmise the inner workings from observations and measurements we can make from the outside. "How it really works" and a myriad of derivative questions stimulate detailed and complex scientific observations. The latter, in turn, make it possible to ask even more sophisticated questions, which generate still more data and so on.

Some modern physicists regard "mind-brain" and "mass-energy" to be similar (perhaps even identical) problems in different versions. In physics, the system of measurement determines the inferred nature of the phenomenon observed—light is *both* a wave function *and* a quantum energy function depending on the system of measurement, and there is no way to resolve this paradox. In the life sciences, anxiety can be observed as a physiologic function or as a subjective state of being, a mental state. Are they the same? Are they different? Does either one cause the other? We have come to one of the central and major sources of our problem: the science of the mind and the science of the body use entirely different languages, instruments, and methods of observation and measurement; they use different conceptual models, which are formulated at very different levels of abstraction. With few, if any, exceptions, information in one realm (physiology) is not directly translatable into that of the other (psychology). Our images of "how it works" (theoretical models) are so different in the two sciences as to seem irreconcilable; they are as different as the systems of observation and measurement used in the two sciences.

So, the mind-brain (body) problem remains with us. It has occupied the attention and energies of philosophers from centuries past to the present. Scientists interested in the nervous system often find themselves in the middle of the ongoing debate about whether mind and brain are best regarded as separate entities (dualism) or whether they constitute a single entity (monism). It is not always possible, when the ultimate truth remains obscure, to separate logical cognitive processes from emotionally tinged beliefs even in the most rigorous discourse. Still, neuroscientists and clinicians working in the health field must deal with practical problems daily and must arrive, at least tentatively, at heuristic perspectives to guide and provide a rationale for their work. As should be clear, it is in this spirit and from an empirical clinical perspective, rather than an abstract philosophical one, that I propose in this volume to tackle the mind-brain problem.

Basic Assumptions

To begin the task, let me make explicit the general bias with which I approach it. *The basic assumption is that the brain is the organ of the mind; in other words, that the brain subserves the collection of mental functions that we call "mind," including those functions whereby the individual negotiates transactions with his or her social environment.* At the same time, the brain acts to regulate, and is in turn responsive to, functions of the rest of the body. In a broader sense, then, "mind" reflects the function not only of the brain but also of the entire body acting through its effects upon the brain. Society, mind, brain, and body can be regarded as a spectrum or series of functional systems that are in open, two-way communication for transfer of energy and information at each interface (see figure 1.1).

To be more focused and pragmatic, let me refer to Steven P. R. Rose's (1978) discussion of "dialectical materialism" as an

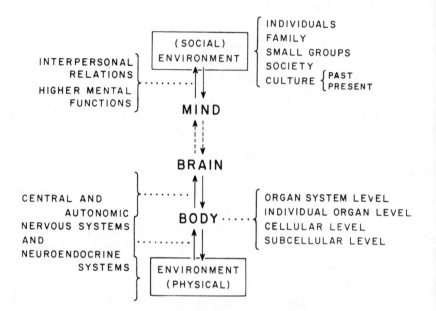

FIGURE 1.1

Model of a Person in a Biopsychosocial Environment: A Series of Communicating Systems and Subsystems

SOURCE: Reprinted from M. F. Reiser "Changing Theoretical Concepts in Psychosomatic Medicine," From *American Handbook of Psychiatry,* ed. Silvano Arieti, vol. IV. © 1975 by Basic Books Inc., Publishers. Reprinted by permission of the publisher.

approach to an exemplary "mind-brain" problem confronted in neuroscience, namely, the relationship between the firing of particular hypothalamic cells and the experience of anger. Rose points out that the reductionist would say the firing of these hypothalamic cells causes the sensation of anger, whereas the dualist would say that the mind, wishing to produce the manifestation of anger, causes the hypothalamic cells to fire, and that the body then responds according to "automatic blind-pilot" landing mechanisms.

For the dialectical materialist (at least my sort of dialectical materialism) the firing of the hypothalamic cells is anger; that is, 'anger' and the 'firing of particular hypothalamic cells' are statements that describe the same phenomenon at different hierarchical levels of discourse (Rose 1978, p. 364).

It is possible to describe the phenomenon in either mind language or brain language, each language system being valid and complete at its own level. "The 'cause' of the anger may be a perceived insult to the individual's experience; the 'cause' of the hypothalamic cells' firing is the antecedent firing of certain other cells, inputs from the sensory system, etc." (Rose 1978, p. 364). Mistakes and confusion result from attempts to locate causes at one level with respect to consequences at the other level. Rather, it is necessary to map events at one level onto events at the other, each described in its own terms. "The task of neurobiology becomes the identification of the translation rules that map mind events onto brain events, psychology onto physiology—the discovery at each level of the necessary, sufficient, and exclusive correlates of events at the other" (Rose 1978, p. 364).

The Need for Intermediate Conceptual Templates

Following in a similar vein, von Bertalanffy's earlier discussion (1964) of this very same problem led me to think that what we need is an "intermediate conceptual template," a template that would be isomorphic with both the biological and the psychological realms, which are not themselves directly isomorphic with each other. Such an intermediate conceptual template would be capable of communicating on one "surface" with the psychological realm about concepts concerning meanings and also capable of communicating on the other "surface" with the biological realm about concepts concerning matter or energy. Perhaps a helpful (partial) analogy can be provided by referring to an actual intermediate template, namely the ribosome, which articulates (communicates) with the genetic code of messenger RNA. The genetic code (sequence of bases on the double helix) supplies instructions for assembling amino acids into proteins in particular ways that are ultimately expressed in terms of a different realm. For example, ribosomes in the iris

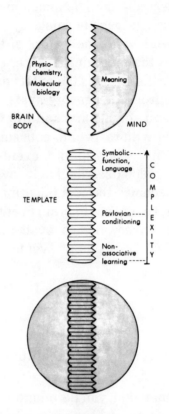

FIGURE 1.2
An "Intermediate Conceptual Template"

of the eye, reading the genetic code instructions, assemble amino acids in a way that finds expression in the realm of color —blue, brown, or green eyes, as the case may be. Stated in still another way, what we need is a conceptual Rosetta stone that could be used to relate, translate, and transpose understanding based on data notated and organized according to one code (psychology) with understanding based on data notated and organized in the other code (physiology). Stephen Toulmin, in discussing this idea, suggested using the term "conceptual transducer." I have tried to depict such a conceptual template schematically in figure 1.2.

As indicated earlier, I shall attempt to work toward a more satisfactory understanding by approaching each realm—mind and brain—separately, in its own terms, and then tracking data from the two in parallel (a "dual-tracking" system). We can hope that the parallel paths will ultimately lead to intermediate bridging concepts. Of course, such a conceptual template as I envision is not now conceivable in its entirety. That is, we cannot hope at present even to imagine a template that would encompass the full range—from the simplest to the most complex—of mental functions. But small, important segments of such a template do seem potentially within reach, including some segments involving complex phenomena (neurobiology of stress). Even more immediately promising are studies of relatively simple cognitive functions in experimental animal models. Here I am referring to the trailblazing work of Kandel and his associates on the changes that occur in single neurons of the marine snail *Aplysia* during and after "learning" of a simple Pavlovian aversive conditioned response (Kandel 1978; see also chapter 9).

From the psychological vantage point, Kandel and his associates observe learning behavior and describe it in the language of learning theory; from the biological vantage point, they observe a cascade of intracellular chemical reactions and describe them in the language of cell biology. Even microscopic changes in cell structure have been reported.

In these studies, behavioral and cell biological data do converge on one small but critically important segment of the more complex conceptual template that some of us envision. The conditioning (learning) data on one "surface" of the segment "speak" to psychology; the biochemical and anatomical data on the other side "speak" to biology. It is not difficult to apprehend the idea of unitary principles underlying both aspects of the events under study. By so doing, I believe it will be possible to attain a previously unattainable depth of understanding.

Based on earlier studies of nonassociative learning (habituation and sensitization) Kandel stated in 1978:

Those of us working in the field find it encouraging to think that we are on the right road and that by taking several large reductionist steps backward, cell biologists have begun to redirect the study of learning to new paths, to where the footing is surer. As a result one can now begin to take some small but confident steps forward (p. 73).

Such steps have been taken (Kandel and Schwartz 1982; Kandel 1983; Bailey and Chen 1983). In the First Annual Elvin V. Semrad Memorial Lecture, entitled "Psychotherapy and the Single Synapse," Kandel (1979) said:

When I speak to someone and he or she listens to me, we not only make eye contact and voice contact but the action of the neuronal machinery in my brain is having a direct and, I hope, long lasting effect on the neuronal machinery in his or her brain, and vice versa. *Indeed, I would argue that it is only insofar as our words produce changes in each other's brains that psychotherapeutic intervention produces changes in patients' minds.* From this perspective the biological and psychological approaches are joined (p. 1037, italics added).

But surely, you will say, it is a long way from acquisition of a conditioned reflex in *Aplysia* to the communicative transactions involved in psychotherapy and psychoanalysis. And I will agree. But still I believe we can make a timely and worthwhile start in the right direction by seriously considering the most complex psychological data we know about and reexamining the nature of both the psychoanalytic process and the data it yields. Admittedly, this will be an abrupt shift to the region of the hoped-for "conceptual template," maximally distant from the regions associated with studies on the cell biology of "educated" *Aplysia* neurons. But, keeping in mind the conceptual dangers of forgetting or ignoring that fact, perhaps a base for future progress can be established by taking a "reductionist step backward" to reexamine and rethink some raw data and some elementary clinical concepts from psychoanalysis and then to think about them in the context of modern neurobiology.

C H A P T E R 2

The Dual-Track

Approach

IF, as discussed earlier, what we know of one domain cannot
be directly articulated with what we know of the other, and if
it seems unlikely that mental and biological processes as such
may ever be understood in the same terms, why care so much
about this interface between psychoanalysis and neurobiology? My intent in asking this rhetorical question is to call
explicit attention to an extremely important but often overlooked reason for taking up the challenge. It is that psychoanalytic data are increasingly being ignored or dismissed
as irrelevant by many neurobiologists AND that neurobiologic
data are increasingly being ignored or dismissed as irrelevant
by many psychoanalysts. How did this come about? How is it
to be understood? The situation bears heavily on the future of
psychoanalysis, inasmuch as it has far-reaching implications
for the proper place and future role of psychoanalysis as a
science that can and should be a contributing participant in the
rapid progress that is taking place all along the frontiers of the
life sciences.

The Relationship between the Disciplines

In discovering psychoanalysis, Freud developed a method of immense power for the study of human mental function—a method not only powerful but *unique,* in that it provides access to quintessential aspects of the human's inner life—aspects that are inaccessible to any other method. Freud's discoveries changed for all time society's fundamental concept of human nature. Ironically, in its very strengths lie the problems of psychoanalysis in relating to the natural sciences. The psychoanalytic process yields subjective data, which are acquired by introspection and communicated within the context of private dyadic relationships. These relationships, as implied by Isakower's concept of "the analytic instrument" (Balter et al. 1980; Malcove 1975), are asymmetrical in that the psychoanalytic process depends on the interaction between two affectively toned memory systems that are asymmetrically tuned, differently motivated, and differentially subject to transference and countertransference distortions. And if that were not enough, add the fact that the process is ordinarily carried out in the absence of veridical (i.e., electronic tape) recording, resulting in reports that are dependent on retrospective recall and subject to unintentional distortions that render them unreliable in the usual sense of the word. Indeed, all of the above constitute serious but hopefully not insurmountable problems. However, biologists may react more negatively to these problems. They may conclude that virtually all information and ideas generated in the course of psychoanalytic work are without value because they consider the methodological context of their origin to be flawed. Although this conclusion may have some validity, it is certainly not entirely correct. To show that the latter assertion is so—and to remedy the problems that do exist—is the burden, but also the challenge and the opportunity, of the discipline of psychoanalysis. If, as many of us believe, precious information is contained in the "crude ore" of data produced by the psychoanalytic process, methods must be developed to extract and refine it. However, as has been pointed out by George Klein (1976), it is crucial that any such methods not seriously distort, trivialize, or otherwise diminish the fundamental core or essence that makes the information valuable in the first place. I concede that this is a formidable challenge but believe that confronting and dealing with it will be justified by the potential results.

On the other side, as already mentioned, an increasing number of psychoanalysts are inclined to regard biological data as irrelevant to psychoanalysis. This inclination traces in part to the fact that metapsychological theory was strongly influenced by, and retains recognizable residues of ideas and postulates from, Freud's (1895) "Project for a Scientific Psychology." Critics of metapsychological theory hold that the idea of a connection with or base in biology is unrealistic since the "nineteenth-century physiology" upon which the "Project" was based is now known to be incorrect and out of date. Metapsychology, these critics say, has led the discipline astray, and psychoanalysis should rather be regarded as a nonbiological discipline. They assert it to be a discipline that deals exclusively with meanings and motives that are disclosed in the psychoanalytic dialogue and that are for all practical purposes unconnected to brain-body. But the psychoanalytic process as a mental process, they concede, depends on the presence of functioning brains in living persons.

This concession constitutes an important "exception" in my opinion—it is not easily treated as a throw-away. Of course, Freud's thinking about mental mechanisms was influenced by the intellectual and scientific context in which it arose, but the validity of the mental mechanisms he described and of the theoretical constructs he proposed to explain his psychological data can and should be judged within (and in terms of) their own domain—that of psychology. They should stand or fall independent of "state of the physiologic art" of his time. Context of origin should not be used as grounds for acceptance or rejection of ideas, that is, in the context of justification. I agree fully that the data of psychoanalytic process tell us about meanings and motives, not about molecules, ions, neurotransmitters, and the like. However, I do not agree that this leads to the conclusion that psychoanalysis, with its insights into meanings and motives, will not or cannot enrich and be enriched by brain science. Such a conclusion, like the one discussed earlier, I find to be partially but certainly not wholly correct.

In my view, serious students of behavior in each of the two domains—biological and mental—are inclined to reject the whole in rejecting some parts. That is, they tend summarily to dismiss valuable data and ideas from the other domain along with the aspects of it they find objectionable or "irrelevant."

Freud abandoned the "Project" and chose not to publish it. He was not satisfied that he could make it work with the neurophysiologic knowledge base available. He decided to confine his work—method and theory—to the domain of psychology. You will remember that the "Project" was published posthumously and not on his volition.

But there are new neurobiologic facts to contemplate now—information that was inaccessible to Freud. And remember, although Freud took the lead in abandoning nineteenth-century physiology, he did so without giving up hope and "belief" that brain science would ultimately provide relevant and useful explanatory information. It is unlikely he would dismiss or turn away from the neurobiologic information that is now available one hundred years later, in this ninth decade of the twentieth century. Still, as I tried to make clear earlier, *all* of the neurobiologic knowledge now available would not fulfill the dream of unified understanding of mind and brain-body in the same set of terms and concepts.

What, then, do I wish to suggest?

Developing the Dual-Track Approach

As mentioned earlier, I wish to suggest an approach to the interface between mind and brain-body—an approach based on the explicit recognition that the realm of mind, which deals with meanings, and the realm of brain-body, which deals with matter and energy, are separated by a composite series of semantic, conceptual, and methodological discontinuities.

In the absence of a Rosetta stone or intermediate conceptual template, psychoanalysis surely should be able to participate in a significant way in the immediate task of identifying the translation rules that map psychology onto physiology (Rose 1978). After all, the full range and depth, the subtleties and gross complexities of human mental life, constitute the primary subject matter of psychoanalysis. Indeed, psychoanalysis ranks high among the psychological disciplines in the capacity to identify the meaningful and important mind events which are to be ultimately mapped onto brain events.

As pointed out by E. O. Wilson (1977), disciplines in science can be regarded as standing in dichotomous pairs: parent discipline and antidiscipline. For every "parent" discipline, there exist one or more antidisciplines which are usually narrower in scope. For example, for social sciences there exist psychiatry and psychoanalysis; for psychiatry and psychoanalysis, neurobiology; for neurobiology, cell biology; for cell biology, molecular biology; for molecular biology, physical chemistry, and so on. In each case the "antidiscipline" serves to generate creative tension in the parent discipline by challenging the precision of its methods and claims, by forcing new ideas and approaches, leading to the modification of insights. The antidiscipline can revitalize and reorient the broader field. On the other hand, being narrower in scope, it does not aid in creating a broader, more meaningful conceptual framework or in enriching paradigms. The latter capacities rest with the parent discipline. The two related disciplines should interact productively, given their different capacities as well as the creative tension between them. In the case of psychoanalysis and neurobiology, Kandel (1979, p. 1029) says, "Although neurobiology can provide key insights into the human mind, psychology and psychoanalysis are potentially deeper in content. The hard-nosed propositions of neurobiology, although scientifically more satisfying, have considerably less existential meaning than do the soft-nosed propositions of psychiatry."

From all of this I conclude that it will be worthwhile to work toward deeper understanding by approaching each realm—mind and brain-body—separately and then tracking the data from the two in parallel—a dual-track approach. For a mutually productive interaction to develop out of the dichotomy, psychoanalysis can and should fill its functions as the parent discipline: First, it should generate questions for neurobiology (its antidiscipline); that is, it should indicate where important questions lie. And, second, it should be prepared to listen, to hear answers, and on the basis of the answers, to rethink concepts and paradigms.

In parts II and III of this book I will attempt to illustrate how this dual-track approach might work, going back to square one —to "start"—and working directly from clinical process data on the psychoanalytic side.

My thesis, to be developed in part II, will be that one promising way for investigators and scholars on the psychoanalytic side to enable the initiation of such interaction would be to go back to a phenomenological study of the process, method, and primary clinical data, as independent of theory and metapsychological constructs as possible. By this I am suggesting the investigators (1) study the psychoanalytic process itself, describing it in operational terms; and (2) reexamine and describe in case material the nature of the clinical data it yields. In part II, detailed excerpts from a psychoanalytic treatment will be presented to illustrate how important questions—in this instance, regarding aspects of memory function—can be generated from clinical process data. I should add parenthetically that some of these questions might be answered within the psychoanalytic domain itself. Part III presents data culled from sectors of neurobiology, selected because they may be regarded as relevant to the questions generated by the psychoanalytic data.

Following the parallel tracking, we can then probe for the possibility of mutually productive "dialogue" between the two data sets. The raw data of the psychoanalytic process will supply the data set from the mental realm. The psychoanalytic data will suggest functional patterns and principles that obtain in the mental realm. The data set from neurobiology will supply observations of actual structures and actual physiologic events involved in the realm of brain function. The latter observations suggest functional patterns and principles that obtain in the biologic realm. Since it is the brain that enables mental function, surely we can *expectantly examine* the two sets of patterns and principles for mutualities and resemblances. This is explicitly what I mean by mutually productive dialogue between the data sets.

As you will see, the probes will raise many more questions than can be answered. And what "answers" there will be will not be direct, nor will they show a one-to-one, point-for-point fit. I suggest that the reader approach this phase of the "data dialogue" with the same mind-set that psychoanalytic clinicians bring to their clinical work: sensitivity to analogies, homologies, metaphors, approximate patterned resemblances, approximate and partial signifier-to-signified relationships, and so on. I am suggesting a special way of thinking about questions that arise in the course of the probes, a pattern of thinking that may at first glance seem—indeed, may actually be—scientifically unorthodox. But such probes could be productive if they can sharpen questions on both sides and if they can point out worthwhile directions for further work in each domain. In turn, new data could be tracked and probed for further dialogue that could deepen understanding and bring us closer to achieving a rational, clinically informed, empirical perspective.

Part II

MIND

THE

PSYCHOANALYTIC

SIDE

CHAPTER 3

The Nature of

the Psychoanalytic

Process

THE TERM "psychoanalysis" as currently used has three referents: (1) a method of treatment, (2) a method of investigating
human mental processes, and (3) a psychological theory. The
first two relate to two different goals which are served by a
single process—the psychoanalytic process. It should be helpful to spend some time examining the nature of that process in
order to understand the kind of information it generates. To do
so, it is necessary to look at the process in the only context in
which it actually occurs, namely, in the therapeutic situation.
In this section, I shall attempt to extract the essence of the
"process" from its broader generic context of theory and treatment. Case material as well as references to and discussions
of theoretical and technical issues are all organized (biased)
with the express intent of clarifying the fundamental essence

of the psychoanalytic process and its rationale as I understand it. Hopefully, this method of organization will facilitate an appreciation of the nature and the richness, as well as the limitations, of the data the process provides. Without such appreciation, serious study of the relationship of clinical psychoanalytic data to data from other clinical and from basic biomedical sciences may not seem feasible or promising. On the other hand, it may well turn out that quite the opposite is the case. If so, there is much to be done.

The "Talking Cure"

In addressing the fundamental nature of the psychoanalytic process and the data it generates, I find myself first turning to old questions that are being asked again—and with increasing frequency—in the current era of biochemical psychiatry: Why should talking be expected to help? How can it be of help in alleviating the forms of human suffering and discomfort that patients bring to psychoanalysts, psychiatrists, and other mental health professionals? If we expect talking to make a difference, there must be a rationale for that expectation.

Freud's concept of psychoanalysis as a therapy was based on a theory of psychogenesis, namely, that psychological factors played an etiologic role in the pathogenesis of neurotic symptoms, behaviors, and character traits. The theory in essence regards neurotic symptoms as originating primarily, though not necessarily exclusively, in psychic conflict. Conflict, a familiar concept in psychology, refers, of course, to a condition in which two opposing and incompatible motives are simultaneously active. ("You can't have your cake and eat it too.") Conflict can be rationally resolved by totally repudiating one side, or by compromise—partially relinquishing or trading off parts of opposing dispositions to action—so far, nothing new in that.

The psychoanalytic theory of pathogenesis adds a crucially significant element. It is that in the case of psychological pathogenic conflict, the opposing motives (or wishes) are not recognized nor are they directly accessible to recognition in consciousness. Since the patient is not and cannot be aware of the nature and extent of the opposing motives, the conflict is not amenable to resolution by rational cognitive processes. Unresolved and actively barred from conscious awareness, the incompatible dispositions are nonetheless considered to remain active, that is, to continue to press for expression. Under these circumstances, the neurotic symptom, behavior, or character trait is thought to develop as a *symbolic representational compromise,* which simultaneously expresses both of the opposing motive forces but *in a form that escapes conscious recognition.* The major hysterical conversion symptom serves as the prototypical example: hysterical paralysis of the arm may simultaneously represent an unrecognized impulse to use the arm for murderous intent *and* "appropriate biblical" punishment for it.

The rationale for the psychoanalytic process as treatment, then, is that it is a process conceived to be capable of making the previously unrecognized (hence, pathogenic) conflictual ideas and motives accessible to consciousness by allowing them to find expression in recognizable form. It then becomes possible for the patient's rational, realistic, mature intellect to appraise, evaluate, repudiate, or compromise as appropriate, and so to resolve the conflict that had been causing the symptom. But the process of bringing the content of the conflict and the defenses associated with it into consciousness does not in itself achieve resolution. What it does, rather, is to give the patient access to the previously inaccessible data needed for the difficult and often painful work of resolution. The latter requires more than just access to information; it also requires the cognitive and emotional strengths and capacities to *understand* the nature and origin of the conflict, that is, the reasons for the problem having been "banished" from consciousness and held "in repression" in the first place. The goal of the

33

analytic work is to clarify unconscious resistances and defenses as well as content, in order to achieve awareness and understanding; resolution is then up to the patient.

This introduces another critically important aspect of the theory: the unresolved pathogenic conflict is considered to have started in childhood (the "infantile neurosis"). At that time the conflicted thoughts and motives could have posed an overwhelming danger situation, since the child would have been unable to cope with the motivational forces if they had had access to the motor systems of body and could thereby gain expression in action—in actual deeds. The young child's mental apparatus is immature, relatively undeveloped, and incapable of advanced cognitive processes (e.g., Piaget has shown that formal abstract thinking becomes possible only in adolescence). Further, in childhood, the capacity for control of impulses and delay of gratification is quite limited. As a matter of fact, the impulses that originally confronted the child might very well have been overwhelming and dangerous in reality if allowed full expression. For example, consider a primitive impulse to kill a parent whom the child loves and totally depends on for survival. On the other hand, the adult, possessed of a mature and well-developed mental apparatus—capable, for example, of mature cognitive function and high frustration tolerance—when given in therapy a "second chance" to resolve the conflict, should be able to confront it without danger of being overwhelmed and to work out a more mature, nonsymptomatic resolution.

But there is still more to it. The process involves more than exploring unfamiliar territory under the tutelage of an experienced guide. The critical additional element is the transference. It warrants discussion at this point. Transference refers to the mental mechanism or process whereby feelings, attitudes, and expectations which one holds, or formerly held, in relation to an important person are displaced or transferred onto another (second) person with whom one has formed a meaningful relationship. For example, trusted and respected teachers become heir to feelings that were originally directed to trusted and respected parents; so, too, it often is between employee and employer, mentee and mentor, and, of course, patient and physician. Clearly, the circumstances of psychoanalytic treatment are such that they are particularly conducive to and serve to amplify this phenomenon. The analysand, who comes regularly and frequently over extended periods of time, shares intimate feelings and reminiscences from the earliest and most meaningful relationships of his or her past and current life, as well as expectations and hopes for the future. Intense emotions and emotionally colored attitudes and expectations inevitably develop and are transferred onto the analyst as the process progresses. In fact (in properly conducted psychoanalytic process), they ripen eventually into a special form of the phenomenon called the "transference neurosis."

In the transference neurosis, the analysand transfers onto the analyst virtually all the emotional and ideational components of the original neurotogenic conflicts that are rooted in early experiences and relationships with key figures such as parents and parent surrogates. When this occurs, the feelings are experienced by the patient as intense, alive, vibrant, and real; feelings such as love, hate, desire, distrust, envy, and suspicion may come alive in the relationship. A crucial point: the analyst is able to help the patient to understand that the intense emotions he* is experiencing as real are in fact ones that have been revived and reactivated. Though they are current, they more properly belong to critical experiences and events that took place earlier in life. It is the experiencing of the difficult, often painful, and tumultuous emotions simultaneous with the intellectual understanding of their archaic origins that provides the perspective whereby the analysand can achieve enough emotional and intellectual distance to "work through" the conflict—that is, to gain mastery of the affects, and independence from the blind motivations that have been stemming from old, previously unrecognized motives and manifesting themselves in symptoms, symptomatic behaviors, and traits.

*Since there is no single word in the English language to denote "he/she," the masculine form will be used throughout the book to avoid the awkward form.

In summary, the theory considers the core neurotogenic conflicts:

1. To have been originally experienced in childhood, to have generated the "infantile neurosis," and to have been embedded in affectively bound memories of contextual developmental life experiences;
2. To have been "forgotten" along with the associated memories as the result of an active psychological process of defense (i.e., actively held out of consciousness by repression and other defenses in order to avoid psychic pain);
3. To have been expressed (represented) in unrecognized form as symptoms—symptomatic behaviors and character traits;
4. To have been transferred (displaced) onto the relationship with the analyst—with the transference neurosis replacing the symptom neurosis;
5. And to be amenable to "working through" when experienced in the transference neurosis and thereby capable of nonsymptomatic resolution by mature cognitive process.

The Special Nature of the Data

The technique of free association serves as the "linchpin" of the psychoanalytic process. One fundamental assumption underlies its use. It is assumed—and clinical experience supports the assumption—that if the patient enters into an agreement with the analyst and does his best to follow the rule of free association, the repressed conflicted motives, and ideas that stem from them, will press for representation in his mind and eventually find expression in his verbalizations. The main features of the contract are (1) to come regularly for sessions of prescribed length; (2) to relax and permit thoughts, ideas, and images to come to mind—without any attempt to control them or in any way judge their possible relevance or therapeutic value; and (3) to verbalize these thoughts as freely as is humanly possible. The use of the couch and positioning of the analyst out of the direct line of vision of the analysand serve to facilitate relaxation and to reduce external sensory input, making it easier for the patient to attend to ideas coming from within. Optimally, the patient's state of mind settles into a level of increased inward, and reduced outward attention—very much like that which obtains in mild drowsiness and states of mind in which reveries and daydreams flourish. The importance of achieving this special state of mind for the psychoanalytic process cannot be underestimated.

The analyst on his part also works with a particular mental set. Freud described it as free-floating, hovering attention—a passively receptive but cognitively active mode of listening. The analyst's frame of mind in listening reciprocates that of analysand as the latter communicates ideas that are coming to mind from within.

Optimal work in the psychoanalytic situation occurs when each of the participants achieves an appropriate state of mind. Under these conditions, ideas stemming from the repressed conflictual motives will manifest themselves in the analysand's free associations and be "heard" by the analyst but—and this is critically important to understand—in special ways. Their form and content are at the beginning and for the most part unfamiliar and unrecognizable to the analysand but *are* understandable (through "decoding" or "translation") to the analyst. Special training has prepared him to "hear" and understand communications that are conveyed largely in the "primary process" mode (see chapter 7). It should be noted here that these primary process communications are embedded, somewhat like code words and signals, in the ongoing text of the conventional secondary-process speech of the analysand. These signals occasionally may evoke images and fantasies in the analyst's mind and under optimal conditions these can serve to facilitate both cognitive and empathic understanding of the analysand.

As the analyst discerns meanings and begins to understand "the emergent messages," he interprets them to the analysand. These interpretative interventions are for the purpose not only of sharing his understanding with the analysand but also of teaching the analysand to "hear" the messages too, thereby enabling him to follow and appreciate the meaning and significance of ideas as they emerge. As the work progresses, the analysand learns to attend to ideas in this analytic way. Metaphorically, the analyst can be thought of as an experienced and skilled guide who accompanies the analysand into unexplored territory and in so doing both guides and educates him, enabling him eventually to be able to follow and understand the contents of previously inaccessible territories in his mind.

In a more complicated but more important metaphor, Isakower conceived of an "analytic instrument"—a functional interactive mental process being transacted by and between the two participants (Balter et al. 1980). He thought of the instrument as being constituted anew in each analytic session and functioning as an amalgam (semiautonomously from each of the participants) for the duration of the hour, after which it would be dismantled to be reconstituted at the start of the next session.

The special qualities of this dialogue in which the mental activities of analyst and analysand interact in this special way make it unique and distinguish it from all other forms of dialogue. To overlook this fact is to miss a central point—a point that explains why the "raw data" does not lend itself readily to conventional objective methods for study of communication and content analysis. This special character shapes the raw data that the process yields for study.

This, to be sure, identifies a big problem—one that may in large part account for the fact that psychoanalysis as a discipline has in its development followed paths that are seemingly so divergent and separate from those taken by other behavioral sciences and by neurobiology. *If psychoanalysis is ever to be brought into productive apposition with these other disciplines, it will be necessary to develop more appropriate methods to process and study its data, ways that will make it possible to exploit the richness of these data more fully and effectively.* This is axiomatic:

I am convinced that, in experimental sciences that are evolving, and especially in those as complex as biology, discovery of a new tool for observation or experiment is much more useful than any number of systematic or philosophic dissertations. Indeed, a new method or a new means of investigation increases our power and makes discoveries and researches possible which would not have been possible without its help (Claude Bernard 1864, p. 171).

Psychoanalytic process and the raw data it can yield seem to me to be vital phenomena crying out for study in their own right. Can we find and/or develop the right methods? First, some data—then, hopefully, some ideas about where and how to start the quest.

CHAPTER 4

Carol

Part 1: Excerpts from Analysis

CAROL, a thirty-four-year-old, white businesswoman, came to psychoanalysis because of an inability to fall in love and marry. She was attractive to and interested in men, but each time a man became "romantic" she would find herself irritable and "bitchy," then anxious and angry as if she were being attacked. Finally she would provoke arguments and a breakup, only to start the cycle again with a new man. The phobic avoidance qualities embedded in this repetitive pattern of behavior, which had successfully defended her against marriage, seem clear. It was reinforced by other phobic behaviors, two of which were connected with intimacy. First, she had what she called "a thing" about damp terry cloth. If she was sharing quarters with another person and reached for an after-shower towel that happened to be damp because the other person had used it, she would shudder with revulsion, throw it down, and feel enraged. Second, the sensation of contact with semen was unbearable to her and she could enjoy intercourse only if the man wore a condom.

She also realized that whenever she did become seriously involved with a man she would have to bring him home to meet her family. She had a vividly detailed fantasy about what would happen. The family would all be seated around the kitchen table. In the course of the conversation her young man would make a "terrible" grammatical error and her family would be horrified that Carol would have chosen a person so obviously uneducated and probably from a lower class. While she was aware of the unlikelihood of such an event actually occurring, she was not able to shake an inner conviction that it would, and she consciously avoided and postponed such an encounter as long as possible.

I shall focus now on one interesting psychological issue that emerged in her analysis. It relates to aspects of memory function, namely, to motivated forgetting and remembering. To highlight this issue and to illustrate some aspects of the psychoanalytic process, I shall in this chapter present detailed excerpts from my analytic work with Carol—all related to a single ("nuclear") traumatic event.

When Carol was four-and-a-half years old, her mother died suddenly and unexpectedly while giving birth to Carol's brother. The very last time Carol saw her mother was on a stormy night when she departed for the hospital. Carol's conscious memory was of standing at the window straining to see through the rain-streaked windowpane as Father drove Mother away. Later in the course of the work, we learned that this conscious childhood memory also (instead?) referred to unremembered aspects of the experience, namely, to the emotional storm within the child and the outpour of tears that blurred her view of her mother's departure.

That night Carol was driven by a relative to her unfamiliar maternal grandmother's home, some ninety or one hundred miles away. When the mother died and Carol was told about it, she had an uncontrollable panic and tantrum, demanding that she be taken to her paternal grandmother, with whom she was familiar. Her father drove through the night to get her and took her to his mother's house, where she and her father lived from that time on. The newborn brother was placed in an orphanage, where he stayed until he was three years old. Only then was he brought into the home to live with the father, grandmother, and two of father's widowed sisters. We learned in Carol's analysis that marrying meant to her bringing a new young man (brother) home to join the family—one of the many conflictual roots of her main symptom.

When the three-year-old brother was brought into the crowded home, Carol had to share a bed with him. He still wet the bed frequently and Carol would, of course, be wetted by the urine and the damp bedclothes. Grandmother would cover the wet sheets with a towel!—remember Carol's wet towel "thing" and aversion to being wetted by contact with semen. Additionally, we later learned that the three-year-old "newcomer" to the home made many gross grammatical mistakes, much to Carol's secret delight. Note the resemblance of this to her fantasy about introducing a serious suitor to her family. Still other factors contributed to her reluctance to marry. Her aged grandmother (eighty plus years at the time the patient entered analysis) declared that she wanted to live only long enough to see Carol married and would be content to die after that happened.

Her father never remarried but, rather, continued to live "at home" with his mother and aging sisters. He often said, "I don't need a wife, I have Carol and she is enough." He apparently did have a secret liaison(s?) outside the home. Carol overheard critical and condemnatory moralistic whisperings about this. When she was twenty-two years old, her father died suddenly of a heart attack. Shortly before that she had had a serious romance but had refused marriage, ostensibly because John, her suitor, had been drafted into the army and was scheduled for overseas duty. She had consented to becoming officially engaged the night before John sailed for Europe. There he was mortally wounded in one of the major battlegrounds of World War II. He died in or near Germany.

Carol was knitting a sweater for him (we later learned that she was having a daydream that she was pregnant and knitting a baby garment) when the official notice of his death arrived. Consciously since childhood she had connected her fear of love and marriage with the possibility of pregnancy and death.

She was certain that should she marry it would be her fate to die like mother in childbirth. John had been her first and last romantic involvement.

Interestingly, several years after her fiancé's death, after it had become clear that she was unable to fall in love, she experienced a gradually developing fantasy. "Someday" she would travel to Europe and there she would meet a man and realize she was already in love with him. Their life paths would seem to have been predetermined as if they were "somehow connected" and destined to be reunited in love. She would be able to marry him. In the analysis we learned that when her mother died, she believed that Mother had gone somewhere far away (to Europe?). We also learned that as a child she believed Mother had died (left) to punish her because she (Carol) had been bad—more on this later.

When the patient was thirteen years old, she and her brother on a rainy Sunday afternoon were in the kitchen making tapioca. She put a large pot of boiling water on the refrigerator to cool. Her brother opened the refrigerator door, the pot fell over, and he was seriously scalded. The neighborhood physician who was contacted sent Carol to the drugstore to get an emergency medication to be applied before the ambulance arrived. She "awoke" three hours later, sitting on a bench in the park with a total amnesia for the intervening time. She had had a major hysterical dissociative fugue. She could not even remember the name of the medication she was supposed to get—in fact, she had never been able to remember it, though she had tried many times—a major disturbance of memory. From this incident and the other background material discussed, note for future reference the prominence of the *kitchen* as a scenic background and the repetitive, important aversive references to dampness—damp towels, rain—and to spilled fluids—warm urine and hot water.

Toward the end of her analysis at the age of thirty-eight (twenty-five years after this burn incident), when engaged to be married, but not yet married, she had a series of dreams about overflowing water (burst pipes, sinks overflowing, etc.), as well as a particularly vivid two-part dream stimulated by reading a novel about a girl who had murdered her mother. The girl had a German name, sounding, she thought, like Elsie Schwollen.

In the first part of the dream, she was planning a trip to Europe and wanted to go to a certain city in or near Germany but *could not remember the name.* The travel agent could not help and referred her to another agent. Becoming increasingly frustrated, she asked to have travel guides of Germany. She would look at all the cities listed there, and maybe then she would be able to recognize the name when she saw it. Then the scene shifted, and she was in the *kitchen* of her fiancé's home with *the whole family sitting around the kitchen table.* She was naked but felt no shame or embarrassment. Her brother-in-law-to-be said, "That's a wonderful tan you have." At this point, she felt intensely embarrassed and felt both guilty and ashamed for the first time in the dream. She asked for a robe. Someone handed her (you guessed it) an old ("from the year one") damp terry cloth robe ("Yuck"). But she put it on and replied, "Well, I am tan but not as tan as Danny (her fiancé)." End of dream. In the course of our work with that dream, I commented that the dream was about the inability to remember a name. I thought perhaps in the kitchen part she *was* remembering the forgotten name of the medicine from the burn incident. I wondered if she might not *now* be able to recall it. She did; it was tannic acid, of course.

QUESTIONS FROM PARENT DISCIPLINE TO ANTIDISCIPLINE

Where in the brain and *how* had that memory trace been stored for twenty-five years? *Why* and *how* did it come to be remembered when it did? What is the nature of the processes that make such motivated forgetting and remembering possible? What is the nature of the processes that clued my memory system to the importance of the dream's issue of not being able to remember a name, and linked it *in my mind* to the story of the tapioca incident that I had heard four years previously?

In the analytic work on this dream we surmised that Mother's membranes had probably ruptured prematurely—in the kitchen—and that the patient had been wetted by the warm fluid. I proposed such a reconstruction; the patient thought it was true, although she could not really remember nor could she get outside information to confirm it. Thus, this reconstruction can perhaps be designated a narrative, although certainly not a historical, truth (Spence 1982); that is, the event as reconstructed seems close to having captured the sense of what was very likely encoded in the patient's "psychic reality." We thought that the accident of the spilled hot water in the tapioca incident had probably revived the panic associated with that original occasion and so precipitated the hysterical fugue.

But the patient did now remember with certainty that the day before Mother went into labor, she and Mother had had a big argument on the steps outside the kitchen, an argument about the patient eating between meals—and being too full at mealtime. They moved into the kitchen where the argument continued and Carol kicked Mother in the belly. She was sure of it. Was it a narrative or a historical truth? In either case, in her *mind* it had the power of truth. Ever since that argument she felt she had been the cause of the tragedy.

Part 2: The Subway Phobia

Four years after termination, the patient called, understandably upset because she had developed a new acute symptom —a subway phobia. This symptom was disabling because it prevented her from going to work; her business was so located that the only practical way she could travel to it was by subway. She had now been married for three years, and the marriage was quite satisfactory.

I made an appointment to see her the next day. She began by telling me that when she had married, she had moved to her own apartment, leaving her grandmother (now ninety plus years) with her two aged aunts. Grandma had continued to live

45

even after Carol's marriage, but recently had suffered a fractured hip. The hip had been surgically pinned, and now she was ready for discharge from the hospital. Carol told me (with a few tightly controlled, angry tears) that her aunts and uncle were sending her grandmother to a nursing home, not wanting to care for her any longer. "She'll die there—no one but me seems to care about her, *they* all seem to *want* her to die."

I asked about the exact circumstances under which the phobia had had its onset. It had happened only a few days earlier. Grandmother was in a hospital in the Bronx, and the patient lived downtown near Greenwich Village. Carol was the only one who had conscientiously visited her regularly, and for her the visit involved a long subway ride. On the day the symptom developed, she boarded the train at a station where the tracks were elevated. On this particular occasion she suddenly became acutely aware of the descent into the tunnel—proprioceptively feeling the train's lowering course, as it traversed the street level and then plunged into the dark tunnel below ground. Within an instant, she felt suffocated, perspired heavily, and felt her heart pounding rapidly in her chest. She rushed out of the train at the first stop, ran upstairs onto the street, and gasped for air—"I'll never go down there again!"

As she was telling this, I had difficulty in listening attentively and felt distracted; my mind wanted to wander onto something else. How terrible, I thought, to be inattentive at a time like this. Then I realized that I was being distracted by a *dream*—worse yet! But, not by a dream of mine, I realized; it was one of Carol's dreams, which she had reported early in analysis (seven years before). I felt relieved—that is important, I'll pay attention. Her early analytic dream that I now let return to my mind clearly was one in which she found herself locked in a toilet stall, unable to get out. Feeling suffocated, she awoke screaming for help and experiencing intense panic as in the incident just described. I remembered our work on the dream seven years earlier. It had led to her recounting an actual event that had occurred when she was eight years old (thirty-one years ago).

Her aunt (Mother's sister, who resembled Mother) had taken

her to the cemetery to visit Mother's grave. Carol had to go to the toilet, and her aunt led her a few steps away from the grave site and down a flight of stairs to the ladies room, which was below ground. As she sat in the toilet stall *urinating* (warm liquid), her hand touched the concrete wall, which felt *cold and damp*. She thought, "My mother is just on the other side of this wall. Where did Mother go, is *she* buried alive?" She cried— felt suffocated, anxious, ran out and up the stairs, again just as in the subway incident.

I told her I was remembering a dream that she had had early in analysis and recounted it to her. She had forgotten it but remembered as I retold it. I then commented, "It sounds like your aunts and uncle aren't the only ones who think it 'is time now for Grandma to die!' " She wept, this time openly and copiously, sighed, and then smiled sheepishly. She understood. The nascent phobia was relieved. We could say that a critical complex of painful affects and forgotten memories had been embedded in the phobic structure which now seemed released, unnecessary after recognition and acceptance of a current guilty wish—a wish that was deeply rooted in previously un-resolved nuclear conflicts from her past life.

Note the complexity of the memory processes: (1) in the patient, (2) in the analyst, and (3) in the interaction between the two. Case reports that deal only with the processes in the analysand may be recounting only one part—a solo version— of what is really a two-part piece—a duet.

MORE QUESTIONS FROM PARENT DISCIPLINE TO ANTIDISCIPLINE

Why did I remember the dream first and then the actual event of the visit to the cemetery? Can study of a "dialogue" such as this between the memory systems of analyst and analysand provide any heuristic hints about memory storage, coding, and recall—about the possible role of such memory processes in the pathogenesis of phobia? Can we ever develop methods to capture the complexities of such processes as these?

Comment

The foregoing psychoanalytic account represents an indeterminate mixture of historical and narrative truths as they exist in my mind—having been reconstructed partly from written process notes and partly from my current memory of the analysis. The process notes were of two types. One was the usual kind written at the end of hours. The other was of a type suggested by Isakower: summaries written from memory shortly after significant phases of the work had been accomplished, for example, after the successful analysis of an important symptom. And there were notes written after each of several post-termination contacts, occurring one, four, seven, nine, sixteen, and seventeen years after termination. The personal recollections, which continue even as this is being written many years after the last visit, span a period of twenty-six years since the start of Carol's analysis. Remembrances from a four-and-one-half year psychoanalytic process that ended a little over twenty years ago constitute "crude ore," to be sure. Still, they clearly are useful for highlighting issues such as those I am raising here concerning memory, storage, and recall. And, importantly, they represent data culled from an actual intense and meaningful process of interaction between two people—data that is hard, if not impossible, to obtain in any other way.

I am concerned, though, that the account might leave readers with an oversimplified, partial concept of the analytic process and/or with the impression that this is an unusually interesting but hardly typical product of work with an exceptional "case" —not so! The account illustrates that meaningful essence can be culled from carefully studied psychoanalytic process data. It calls attention to the nature of data reduction processes, which so clearly involve mental processing within the mind of the analyst. These cognitive processes, like the operations in the patient's mind, are by their very nature personal and private in the sense that they cannot be fully explicated, reported, or subjected to tests of reliability and consensual validation as can data in the natural sciences and experimental psychology.

Can they be trusted or taken seriously? I do not know the answer to that question. Clearly I think they can—perhaps in some special way that will make sense. In chapter 2 I discussed the fact that the data of psychoanalytic work do not lend themselves readily, if at all, to the research methods of natural science. Many efforts to make it conform have merely resulted in trivializing the work. I do not wish to argue against continuing serious efforts along these lines. On the contrary, I applaud them and am convinced that real progress is evident in development of methods for utilizing tape-recorded sessions—as well as content analysis and quantification techniques, for example—in ways that promise to yield deeply meaningful, significant, and important results (Dahl et al. 1978; Gill 1981; Gill and Hoffman 1981; Luborsky 1973, 1976; Spence et al. 1978).

But might we not also struggle along a different path, toward processing analytic work in other ways that would preserve the full dimensions of the data and still lend a sense of "face validity" and render it heuristically promising? Working toward that end, the chapter that follows presents some additional detailed work from Carol's analysis. These additional data should dispel any misimpressions of oversimplification in the case report so far. They also illustrate how overdetermined behavior may be—a problem that adds considerably to the difficulties of processing analytic data. At the same time, the additional information enriches and deepens understanding in unique ways that encourage me—and, hopefully, will encourage others—to continue the search for alternate approaches to the study of psychoanalytic process. My hope, of course, is that we might by returning as directly and closely as possible to the immediate data of psychoanalytic process be enabled (subjectively and introspectively) to generate *ideas* that in turn would be amenable to and appropriate for study by more conventional methods, either within or outside the analytic situation.

CHAPTER 5

More about Carol

AT THE END of the last chapter, I expressed the hope that I could enlist at least some optimistic support for persisting in the belief that studies of the analytic process by introspective methods might be expected to generate ideas that could, if we were wise enough, serve as unique leads in the search for ways of understanding a human mind and its relation to the more materially accessible aspects of the person, that is, to brain-body. The way I have chosen to enlist such support is to present additional data from Carol's analysis—data that both complicate and simplify an understanding of her and of the analytic process. That it does these two things simultaneously in a way constitutes the problem. We are limited by the state of the art. Perhaps the state of the art in this work is but another manifestation of the human condition.

Part 3: Secrets

Shortly after her father's death, Carol drifted into an affair with Ken, a man who was married and had a young daughter. Both he and his wife were Catholic, and there would never be any chance of his obtaining a divorce. The relationship with this man, who was about fifteen or twenty years her senior, had developed quite rapidly from a casual friendship at work after he had confided to Carol that he and his wife did not get along and that he had fallen in love with Carol and desperately needed her to maintain a stable life adjustment. For about ten years preceding the start of analysis, she and Ken had met daily for coffee, would spend two evenings a week together, and when the occasion presented itself, would spend weekends together, usually at his country home.

Carol consciously realized that she was in some way filling a place in Ken's life similar to the one she had for her father. Ken, like her father, had an only daughter; there was, however, a reversal in that with Ken she was the secret other woman permitting his relationship to his daughter to be undisturbed. Carol also realized that her attachment in this relationship was a powerful factor in her avoidance of marriage, since she was not open or available emotionally to develop a deep, lasting relationship with an eligible man. She had told only one other person about this secret relationship. Once, during a period of discouragement, she confessed it to her aunt, expecting that her aunt would be dead set against such a relationship and would exert considerable pressure on her to terminate it. Much to her surprise, this did not happen. Rather, her aunt was accepting and objective but pointed out to her that the price she paid for that relationship was being unavailable. Still, she explained that it was not her business to advise, and she reassured Carol that she would understand and stick by her no matter what she did, much to Carol's combined relief and disappointment.

When Carol started analysis, she decided that it was the proper time to break off her relationship with Ken, and in fact, she did this abruptly—and, she felt, firmly—the day before her first analytic appointment, explaining to Ken that there was no point in her investing so much time and money in her treatment if she would, at the same time, continue their relationship. He acquiesced and so it was settled. But at the conclusion of her first analytic hour, she was overwhelmed with panic. As she left the building where my office was located and started to head for home, she suddenly realized that she could not tolerate the notion of being separated from Ken and had to tell him so as quickly as possible and get his agreement to continue seeing her. With mounting anxiety that she would not be able to find him, she hurried to his office building and was able to determine from the pattern of lights in windows of this very large building that indeed somebody was present on the floor where Ken's business was located. Her panic and desperation increased when she found that the building was locked and there was no way to get inside, and his telephone did not answer. For what seemed like many, many hours, she ran desperately and methodically up and down the streets in the neighborhood, looking for his car. If she could find the car, she would know that he was upstairs in his office and could wait for Ken by the car. That actually is what happened. They indeed were reunited in the relationship, which then continued more intensely than ever throughout the first three years of her work in analysis. As a matter of fact, she would meet him for dinner after the majority of her analytic hours, but did not tell me about these meetings until much, much later. The resemblance between her panicky need that night for an instant reunion with Ken and the panic she had the night that her mother died was instantly apparent to her even at the time, although she was unable to control it. Clearly she set it up from the beginning for her relationship with Ken to counterbalance opposing wishes to fall in love and marry someone who would be available. She tried so far as circumstances would permit to neutralize each hour of analysis with a secret meeting with Ken.

Uncovering Secrets

I propose now to recount in some detail three consecutive analytic hours that occurred after the patient had been in analysis for one-and-a-half years. In these hours, she reported for the first time a symptom that she had never talked about in the analysis even though it had been a major source of discomfort to her. The work we did at this time clearly revealed the meaning of this symptom, including the reason for her having kept it secret from me.

The first of these sessions, which was on a Monday, began with her talking about an incident that had occurred during the weekend. She had met Ken in the city and while they were eating dinner, she told him about a vivid dream. *It had come into her mind as they were eating and talking. She had not remembered it until that moment. It was so intense that she had to talk about it immediately,* although she had never before reported or discussed dreams with Ken. This one had occurred the previous night. It was brief.

In the dream, her friend Ann was living with her, and Ann said she was going to kill herself. Carol explained to me that she had not seen Ann for several years—in fact, had lost contact with her as she had with most of her married friends, especially after they have had babies. The last time she had seen Ann was when she visited her in the hospital on just such an occasion. Carol had felt so uncomfortable and strained at that visit that she avoided seeing Ann ever since and refused invitations to have dinner at her home. She went on to talk about another married friend, who has annoyed her by her constant chattering about her children "as if nothing else in the world is important." This second friend, Gloria, had gotten very sloppy and unattractive. The last time the patient had seen her, Gloria was pregnant and was wearing wrinkled clothes; before marriage she had been such a chic, alert, and clever young woman. She added that she dislikes Gloria's husband too. He is so full of self-importance and "acts like the lord of the manor." Carol reflected then that she and her friends had not thought much of Ann's husband at the time Ann married. They felt he was not good enough for her. Among other things, he was about twenty years older and not very stylish. Still, she went on, "Ann has become even more attractive than before, even though she has had three children. For a long time she had hesitated about marrying him, but obviously she had made the right decision for her." At this point, Carol said that she was very puzzled as to why Ann would want to die in the dream. "Certainly I don't have the slightest notion that I would feel that way toward her. It's just that she makes me uncomfortable."

There followed a discussion of the difference between what had happened to Ann and what had happened to Gloria. Carol said without hesitation that she would not possibly want to trade places with Gloria, but it bothered her about Ann because the marriage had worked out so well. *She could not see her or think about her without becoming aware of her own wishes to be married that she has denied and resisted for so long.* It was at this point that she remembered having told her aunt about her relationship with Ken and was puzzled why she did not feel relieved and better after having gotten it off her chest and not having been scolded. "My aunt just firmly pointed out that the longer I let it continue, the harder it would be to break it off. I felt very unsatisfied after that. What in the world could I have wanted her to say? I wanted something but didn't know what. I wonder, is the fact that the age difference between Ken and myself is the same as between Ann and her husband important? Does it have meaning? *Could it mean that I wish something like that for me and Ken?*" I responded by asking if she does *really* wonder about that. She became visibly and intensely upset, raised her voice, and said that she could not ever let herself have such a wish. She thought about how desperately she has fought against it. I pointed out that in the dream, she definitely tried to annihilate this wish that is pressing into awareness. At that point, she reported that *following dinner that evening when she told the dream to Ken, she suddenly became very ill and had to rest a while before she was able to get up and leave the restaurant.* She did not at that moment specify what the illness was beyond saying that it was "like an upset stomach." These comments came at the very end of the session.

The night after that session, she had a dream with which she opened the next session. "I had a crazy dream last night. It won't be possible to make anything of it at all." In the dream, she was at the country home of her employer and his wife, although actually it did not look like his country home. The one in the dream was very vividly surrounded by luscious, luxurious gardens, filled with beautiful flowers and shrubs and enclosed by a vine-covered wall. They were eating breakfast and she said to the boss, "This isn't the room where we usually have breakfast," to which he answered, "No, *the breakfast room has burned.*" Then her boss's wife said something that was replete with literary allusions and asked if Carol understood. She said, "No." She could not understand the wife but did understand the things that her boss was saying. Then the scene shifted in the dream, and she was at a country resort with her cousin Eunice. They had just checked into the resort, and their room was very small and sparsely furnished. They walked down the hall to the elevator. The doors of all the other rooms were open, and she noticed that they were all much larger. In the other rooms, there were shoes everywhere—on the floors and on the furniture. They had to wait for the elevator and Carol became furious and thoroughly annoyed. She decided to go back to her room and put on a bathing suit. Telling Eunice she would meet her downstairs in the lobby, she rushed back to the room to change. Though she was in a hurry, it seemed to take forever. She just could not finish. She got her clothes off very quickly, but could not finish getting into the bathing suit. End of dream.

She began immediately to talk about being so hard to please and to fit for shoes, "because I'm so vain, I suppose." She went on to explain that Eunice had to wear horrible, ugly shoes in order to fit braces (Eunice had polio as a child and has one deformed leg). (Eunice is now married and has had several babies.) Carol fell silent and said that there were no other thoughts about the dream, but mentioned that Ken had called that afternoon and indicated that he was not going to be able to keep their standing date that evening. She was quite annoyed and let him know it. Later she felt bad because he had been under great pressure, and "it's not fair to be mean to him," but when he called back later in the day, though she intended to reassure, again she showed her annoyance and upset him further. I pointed out that she had been very annoyed in the dream waiting for the elevator. "Yes, but that's not anything special, I'm always impatient and annoyed. The building manager where I work is often slow in answering the elevator bell. Sometimes at night, he's locked the building without checking. When that happened, I would be locked inside the building overnight."

She went on to say that this morning, she was impatient and annoyed because the subways were late. When she arrived at work, she could not find the key to her office (locked out). Her boss was in a conference, and she had to interrupt the conference to ask for the key, and that told him and everyone else that she was late. The fact that he did not chide her made her feel even worse. When she got back upstairs, she found that she had had the key in her purse all along, and recognized that she had had a need to show him that she had misbehaved. This guilty need, she thought, was connected with the shoes in the dream. She had been feeling very contrite about being so mean to Ken. She has been thinking she should tell him she would go out to his country home with him for a weekend; that, she thought, might have something to do with shoes. Ken had a friend who has a shoe factory. He can take her to the factory where she can buy shoes wholesale. The factory now has moved to another city. She ought to ride down there with Ken, but that would mean staying with him at a hotel and registering as man and wife, which she does not want to do.

Carol then mentioned that the other day she was in the expensive, upstairs shoe department in a very stylish women's store. The salesperson showed her a perfect pair of shoes, both stylish and comfortable. She seldom has been able to find such a combination. She was ready to tell him to wrap the shoes for her and realized that she had not asked the price. He mentioned a very high figure. "Well, then you had better let it go. I am not psychologically ready to pay that price." I asked, "You said *that* to him?" She asked why I inquired. I answered that it was because "that is what you really want to say to me."

Carol replied to my comment by saying, "Well, there is something bothering me; I was terribly upset after yesterday's hour.

I got panicky. I thought you were encouraging me in my feeling for Ken. All along I felt, though you don't say anything, that you disapprove and feel I should separate from him. Yesterday, I got the feeling that you want to encourage my wish. I don't want to go through all this just to find out that I'm in love with Ken and want to marry him. That's what the strange breakfast room was in the dream. The surroundings have changed and I don't understand them. For a year-and-a-half, I thought you felt one way and now I get the feeling that you may feel the opposite." I replied, "Rather, I was making you aware of the price you have to pay, and you feel you are not ready yet to buy the shoes you wanted on your own, that is, to get your own husband. You can still get them wholesale through Ken. What you haven't realized until now is how expensive it would be emotionally. You haven't until now realized the depth of your attachment. You knew that this was not an ordinary platonic affair. You knew it wasn't a bargain basement where you were shopping, but you didn't know it was the most expensive department upstairs." I went on, "What you want from analysis costs more than you thought. What you couldn't understand, what confused you, was the thought that I, like your aunt, can understand what you feel for Ken without condoning or condemning what you might do. You understand this from the way we work here. Analysis only identifies what the situation is. If I would have any bias or interest, it would only be to help you to a position where you will be able to do what *you* feel will be most satisfactory for you." That was the end of the second of the three hours.

She started the next hour by saying that she did not feel like talking. As a matter of fact, she did not even feel like coming. Probably she said too much yesterday. Parenthetically, she noted that her boss was going to Europe in a few days and would be away for about three months.

I commented that it was interesting that she had dreamed about Ann and Eunice in the same week. Carol went on to remember that one summer instead of staying at her aunt's house, her aunt took her and Eunice to the seashore; they were about twelve years old at the time. (Carol used to spend all of her summer vacations with the aunt and her cousin but usually at the family home and not away.) There was a boy at the shore who was Carol's "boyfriend." She went on to say that Eunice might have been expected to have jealous feelings about it. Instead she was happy and encouraging. When they played kissing games, Eunice arranged for the cards to come out so that Carol always won. "Eunice is so well adjusted, she never experienced any jealousy. You would think she would have it." I commented that not to be jealous when you could be might not be the hallmark of perfect adjustment.

Immediately another incident came to her mind. It was during the summer that she had graduated from college and that John, her fiancé, had been sent overseas. The patient had spent her vacation with her friend Ann, again at the seashore. They had rented a place there. Carol did not do much that summer and mostly sat around knitting army socks. She was always knitting things to send to John. One morning that summer she was sitting on the bed when the doorbell rang. It was a man bringing groceries that her aunt had ordered for them from the city. As he started up the stairs, the patient was suddenly seized with an excruciating pain in her stomach. It lasted off and on for hours. *It was the same pain that she had experienced this past Saturday night while having dinner with Ken.*

She had such attacks frequently after that first bout. Her aunt took her to many doctors, who could not find anything wrong. The last doctor, she said, thought it was probably because she was nervous; and her aunt told the doctor, "Well, her mother died when she was a baby." Carol became furious with her aunt for having told this, and since then had given up on ever getting any relief from it, having seen so many doctors, had extensive X rays and so on, all without a diagnosis. She no longer even mentions it to anybody. I inquired about the nature of the pain. It starts as a dull pain, gradually mounts, reaches a high of almost unbearable intensity, then stops, only to start all over again. *I commented that the first attack had occurred when she was sitting on the bed and the "delivery man" came in, and I wondered if maybe she was spinning a daydream at that time. "What do you mean? Could it be that I was wishing or dreaming that I was married to John and pregnant, knitting for a baby?"* She added that when the telegram came telling that John had been killed, she was in the middle of knitting a sweater that she had never finished. She had never picked up her knitting needles again and has never known why. She agreed with me that she had just come across the reason.

The Tannic Acid Dream Explained

We are now ready to review in more detail the analytic work with the "tannic acid dream." You will recall that this dream occurred almost at the end of her analysis, when she was experiencing vicissitudes of a conflict with a man to whom she was engaged. At one moment they would be on the verge of marriage, the next deciding to break up. Carol had somewhat earlier raised the question of setting a date for termination of the analysis, but nothing had yet been decided about it. There had been many references to conflicts and fears of pregnancy. With high frequency, Carol's thoughts would go back to the night of her panic following her mother's death. Dreams of spilling water began to reappear. In one such dream, there was water all over the bathroom floor, and although the dream was very vague, she had the impression that her mother had spilled it and that her mother was wiping it up.

A few days after this particular dream, she remembered an incident that had occurred around the age of five or six while she was visiting with her aunt and her cousin Eunice. The memory was of having been given an enema by her aunt, feeling intense humiliation and shame as well as physical discomfort, fearing that she would be unable to hold the fluid in. As she described this memory, she experienced the sensation of being suspended on the couch and then amended this to say it was more like she was being swept away or "floated off." Along with that sensation came the thought that the enema experience was connected with pregnancy—being filled up and swollen, water being put in under pressure; then again, she spoke of concern about being unable to hold the water in.

Her mind quickly went back to previous dreams of water spilling and her aversion to the thought of having intercourse without a condom. In this context, it occurred to her as a disconnected and strange, out-of-place thought that there is something that happens to the woman before she goes into labor. She was very vague about this, but "isn't there something about the water breaking?" She recalled now that she had been told that her mother was bleeding for a few days before she went into labor. Carol thought perhaps she had seen something or sensed her mother's anxiety. Recalling again her memory of trying to see through the rain-streaked windowpane, she discussed the question of whether it was actually raining that night or whether this was a memory of tears and blurred vision because of her grief and crying. *She spoke of a particularly strong current feeling that something terrible would be discovered at work or that she had done something wrong or had failed to do something important, and she remembered that as a child, she had been quite concerned that maybe she had kicked her mother, caused the baby to disappear. Now she remembered wanting the baby to be thrown away. Maybe she did do something.* I commented that it may very well have happened that her mother's membranes ruptured at home and that she either saw it or heard about it. In the following hour, she reported the two-part dream, which I will now recount in somewhat greater detail than before.

In the first part of the dream, she was to go somewhere with a group of girls but was traveling alone rather than with them. She went to a ticket agent and wanted to get somewhere in Germany, but could not think of the name of the city. The name of the city was a hyphenated name like Frankfurt-on-Rhine. She thought in the dream that it was something like that but she could not remember it exactly. She and the ticket agent began taking a walk, and he became interested in her and proposed marriage, but she found him unattractive and tried tactfully to let him know that she could never be married to him. Then she was at another ticket agent's office and talked to him. She asked him if he could give her a map or a travel folder about Germany. Maybe in there she could look over a list of places tourists go and find the name of the place she was looking for.

In the next part of the dream, she was at Danny's house in the kitchen. His mother, his sister and brother, and their children were all sitting there around the table. The patient was naked, but this did not seem odd or embarrassing to her or to the others. Her brother-in-law-to-be said to her, "You still have some of your summer tan left." She felt a little tinge of embarrassment over this, but replied that she was a little tanned but not nearly as tan as Danny. Then Danny's sister said, "Don't you want to put on a robe or something?" She said, "Yes," and his sister brought down a terry cloth robe, apologizing that it was old and looked like "it was from the year one." Carol put it on and became very uncomfortable and annoyed because it was damp. Somebody had used it to dry off, and the dampness was a very annoying sensation. She awoke with a shudder. She had the feeling when she awoke that she had had a second dream about a girl who murdered her parents and was startled to recall that the night before she had been reading a book about a girl who murdered her parents.

We first connected her aversion to wet towels and the terry cloth robe to her brother's enuresis. She got interested in the business about names, of not being able to name things. She could not think of the name of the town in Germany. Then she remembered reading a book the night before, but could not remember the name of that. Then we noted the preoccupation in the dream about not being able to remember the name of a town. The name of the book may be something like *Joshua's Vision* and the heroine was named Elsie Schwollen, which is a German-sounding name, and, of course, immediately sounds like it has to do with pregnancy, she added. At that point, she lost interest in working on the dream and seemed to feel that nothing more could be learned from it.

I commented that she seemed to feel about this dream as she did about the names, that something was "on the table" but that she could not get it or catch on. She seemed to be regarding the dream without much interest or hope that anything important would emerge clearly. She acknowledged that was exactly how she felt about all of the things that were stirring at the moment in the analytic work. I asked if she might get interested in the dream again if I introduced the idea that the scene in the kitchen might refer to some actual incident in her life. As I made that comment, a whole series of pictures came into her mind.

First, there was a new memory of standing at the door of the kitchen where her grandmother and aunt were sitting at the table. She told a fib without any idea of what she had to gain by it, and it was over an unimportant matter anyway. Maybe she just wanted attention for something she felt guilty about. Maybe she just wanted to say something to feel included. She remembered a dream with water overflowing from the kitchen sink, and then said, "Of course, my mind goes immediately to that time water spilled and burnt my brother." I commented that she had taken the next step. When I suggested an actual incident, she brought one up and then a whole series of images, superimposed one on the other—the kitchen, water, feeling she had not been truthful. I added that I thought we could now understand better her intense confusion and amnesia about the medicine for her brother when he was burned. Perhaps, I suggested, the confusion that overtook her at that time, in addition to being a reaction to her unconscious urge to hurt him, could have included a return of the panic and confusion that belonged to a scene in which her mother's membranes ruptured. I reminded her that the dream was about a forgotten name and asked then if she could recall the name of the medicine she was supposed to get for her brother. As might be expected, she still could not remember. She said she could remember only that it was not an ointment, that it was some kind of powder used for emergencies, dissolved in water, and spread on like paste. I said then that the forgotten name of the medicine was referred to in the dream and she instantly said, "Of course, it was tannic acid." *Both of us could see clearly that the point of embarrassment in the dream was over the issue of being tanned and not as tan as Danny who, of course, stood for the brother.* (It is not hard to imagine someone asking her if she had been burned too.)

She ended the hour quite stimulated by all this and wondered then why it was that she could not remember ever having eaten in a kitchen. The only time she ever remembered eating in a kitchen was once with cousin Eunice. She was fighting with Eunice over a banana. *Then she added that she could now remember an incident when she was eating cereal on the steps leading to the kitchen and fighting with her pregnant mother about eating between meals and being too full at mealtime. That was the fight that led to her actually kicking her mother in the abdomen and her fear that she had caused her mother's death.*

CHAPTER 6

Memory Storage and Psychoanalytic Process Data

IT IS MY HOPE that by reviewing the foregoing additional material in detail, with all of its ambiguities and redundancies, I have been able to impart some idea of what it is like to confront information that presents itself in this way. The information as I have given it to you is still, of course, at a considerable distance from the "raw data," but it is close enough for you to wonder how to make sense of it, or more accurately stated perhaps, how to explicate the innate sense it may very well seem to make to you. Please bear in mind that I do not propose to deal with it comprehensively or to a point of precise intellectual closure; rather, I want to focus on patterns of memory function that can be discerned in such data.

The patterns themselves are not new; they are the same ones Freud (1900) described in *The Interpretation of Dreams*, specifically in his discussion of the "Dream of the Botanical Monograph." There, you will recall, he suggested that ideas represented in the manifest content of dreams—in this case, "botanical" and "monograph"—could be thought of as nodal points upon which numerous trains of thought converge. The trains of thought are linked in the hypothetical "mental apparatus" by affective associations and woven together around (usually) visual memory traces; these, in turn, are connected with still other thoughts belonging to emotionally related meaningful conflictual events—current, recent, intermediate, and even remote past experiences reaching back to the very earliest experiences capable of registration and retention in memory.

This first investigation leads us to conclude that the elements 'botanical' or 'monograph' found their way into the content of the dream because they possessed copious contacts with the majority of the dream-thoughts, because, that is to say, they constituted 'nodal points' upon which a great number of the dream-thoughts converged and because they had several meanings in connection with the interpretation of the dream. The explanation of this fundamental fact can also be put in another way; each of the elements in the dream's content turns out to have been 'overdetermined'—to have been represented in the dream-thoughts many times over.

The nature of the relation between dream content and dream-thoughts thus becomes visible. Not only are the elements of a dream determined by the dream-thoughts many times over but the individual dream-thoughts are represented in the dream by several elements. Associative paths lead from one element of the dream to several dream-thoughts, and from one dream-thought to several elements of the dream (Freud 1900, pp. 283–84).

He is referring here to the mechanisms of "condensation" and "displacement" (see figure 6.1).

Memory Networks: Storage and Retrieval

What I wish to propose is that exactly the same pattern of memory "storage" that Freud described as underlying the relation of manifest dream contents to latent dream thoughts can

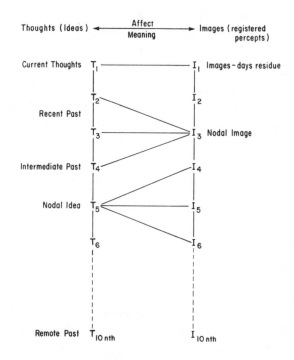

FIGURE 6.1

Relation of Dream Thoughts to Dream Images

This figure diagrams the relationship between thoughts (ideas) and dream images (registered visual percepts) as conceptualized in Freud's discussion of the "Dream of the Botanical Monograph" (see p. 65). Images constitute manifest content of the dream, whereas thoughts and ideas carry the latent (meaningful) content. They are linked by shared affect and meaning. In the diagram thoughts are serially ordered chronologically from current (T_1) at the top to remote past (T_{10nth}) at the bottom of the figure. Dream images and secondary images that arise in the course of free associations likewise are serialized chronologically from current images (days residue) I_1 at the top to historically older ones, (I_{10nth}) at the bottom of the diagram. The figure is designed to illustrate the principle that several thoughts may be rendered as a single image (condensation) and, conversely, that several images may (via displacement) represent a single idea.

be detected not only in an individual dream but also in the patterning of stored memories that underlies the relationship between nuclear developmental conflicts and later enduring and repetitive patterns of adult behavior such as specific neurotic symptoms and character traits. Palombo (1978) has suggested that one function of the dream may be to store or fix memories of events by locating them appropriately in enduring memory systems or "memory trees." While Freud was explicit in stating that neurotic symptoms and dreams were constructed (that is, functioned) identically—to achieve compromise symbolic solutions to otherwise insoluble conflicts—he was not to my knowledge explicit in extending the concept of memory networks displayed in a single dream to a concept of networks that endure longitudinally in time, although it would be surprising to me if he did not implicitly think of it that way.

In any event, such a notion has interesting theoretical implications. For example, it implies that each of us carries somewhere within an enduring core network of stored memories— stored and linked in relation to a shared potential to evoke identical complexes of emotional experience. Such a network would be historically rooted in early and—for the child— cataclysmic events, either real or elaborated in fantasy. As development proceeds, the network would branch out with the occurrence of later events that set the earlier ones into resonance because they posed the same or similar problems. In this sense the later events could be thought of functionally as presenting emotional analogues or homologues of the earlier ones. Traces of such events and issues left encoded in memory then could be thought of as constituting *nodal* points as Freud conceived of them for the individual dream.

Extending the idea in this way also has potentially important clinical implications. It means that adding new elements to the network is an ongoing process. Events occurring currently can and do set earlier ones into resonance, and so link up to and sometimes become part of the network. This would suggest that thoughts emerging as "free associations" could, when they find their way into the core network, then follow it into highly charged (condensed) nodes and the issues they signify. As the encoded issues get closer to earlier epochs, the nodal point ideas would be fewer (more condensed). Such a hypothesis would predict that new recovery of (usually early) significant memories should be facilitated when representations of such highly condensed nodal ideas emerge and are pursued in the course of free association. It would be possible rigorously to test such a hypothesis within the psychoanalytic situation itself (Edelson 1983). Similarly, the latent content (underlying dream thoughts) of any individual dream can be regarded as a potential portal of entry to the entire network. Productive historical analytic work with a dream—leading to new recovery of memories—may signify that the thoughts emerging as "free associations" are ones that have found their way into the core network and so have been able (sometimes with amazing rapidity) to follow into the highly charged (condensed) nodes and the issues they signify.

You have probably already guessed that the idea of spilled water (wetness) is going to be cited here as a prime example of a highly condensed nodal element in Carol's mind. Figure 6.2 depicts the way condensed and displaced nodal images and thoughts are represented in the tannic acid dream.

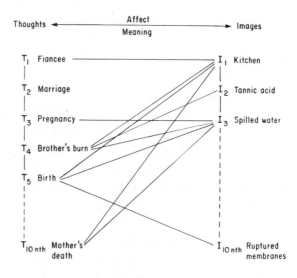

FIGURE 6.2

Relation of Dream Thoughts to Dream Images in the Tannic Acid Dream
This figure depicts the relationship of thoughts (ideas) to images in the "Tannic Acid Dream." It illustrates the mechanisms of condensation and displacement as manifest in nodal images (kitchen and spilled water) and nodal thoughts (brother's burn, birth, mother's death) in that dream.

A brief example of a psychoanalytic technique in working with a dream may help to illustrate a clinical point. In seminars and supervision Isakower taught that a crucial key to unlocking a dream lies in the analyst's searching his own mind for possible links between the meaning of current and past issues in the patient's life as they are represented by common elements of the dream's manifest content—in this way to match ongoing concerns with important issues of the past.

The next step is somehow to engage the patient's interest in this match-up. One way of doing this—that is, to engage the patient's interest in confronting the superimposition of present and past concerns—is by directing attention to the common element of the manifest dream as a starting point for free associating to the dream. The trick is in finding the most promising element(s) to use (part of the art as well as the science). In the tannic acid dream the match between current issues (engagement, impending marriage, and possibility of pregnancy) and past issues (mother's pregnancy, ruptured membranes, and death) was represented by an issue in the dream that was common to both—a forgotten name (of a city in the dream, of the burn medicine in the past). Focusing on a "switch" word may be especially effective. A "switch" word is one that makes sense in each of two contexts, but its connection with only one of the two is usually consciously in the patient's mind. *Tan* was a switch word here. It fit with two time contexts, current and past. Like any manifest element of the dream that connects to both past and current issues it is likely to be located close to a nodal issue. When the common element (forgotten name) was brought into focus and related to both time contexts—the forgotten name of medicine from the burn incident in the past, and the forgotten name of a city in the current dream—*tan* acted as the switch word to tannic acid and permitted the subsequent associations to follow into the core nodal memory network. This led then in further associations to recovery of a highly meaningful and significant new memory (kicking mother in the stomach shortly before her membranes ruptured).

It would be nice to present here a neat, unambiguous diagram of Carol's enduring nodal memory network ("Mnet" scan) and to retrace point for point a path through it from the process material presented in chapters 4 and 5—nice, but not possible! Instead, behold figure 6.3.* What does it have to say? It depicts in a rough, schematic way a central nodal traumatic experience: the death of Carol's mother with all of its surrounding circumstances, which was certainly for the four-and-a-half-year-old child a cataclysmic event. Separation, panic, grief, bewilderment, secret triumph over Mother and Brother, exclusive possession of Father, guilt, fear, dread —all must have been intense and overwhelming. Immediately contiguous events intimately associated with the nuclear experience involved wetness and fluid incontinence, ruptured membranes and tears. Later events (reintroduction of Brother to family) resonating with the same emotional birth-connected issues link again through fluid—incontinence, enuresis, warm urine, wetness, cold urine, damp, clammy terry cloth. Damp, cold terry cloth becomes a nodal point, linked in one direction to pregnancy, birth, grief, tears, and the unwelcome brother, and in another, to semen and the danger of pregnancy. Later the enema experience at the hand of Mother's sister with Carol's crippled cousin present forms another link to the idea of pregnancy and birth—internal body fluid under pressure for release and, finally, the incident in the cemetery, urinary urgency with fantasies of Mother being buried alive. Still later, the burn incident (now the fluid is hot, damaging, and life-threatening) again provides a guilt-provoking link-up with all that has gone before, and the patient again reacts in a cataclysmic way.

We can see in the lower half of the figure a cluster of intimately related nodal points: burns, tears, fluid under pressure, wet, dampness, wet terry cloth, incontinence, semen, being enclosed, suffocated, buried alive. Figure 6.3 shows how the

---

*The temptation to refer to these rough schematic diagrams of Carol's enduring nodal memory network as "Mnet" scans was irresistable. Resemblance of this term to acronyms of more precise, sophisticated technical procedures is intentional—but not to be taken seriously.

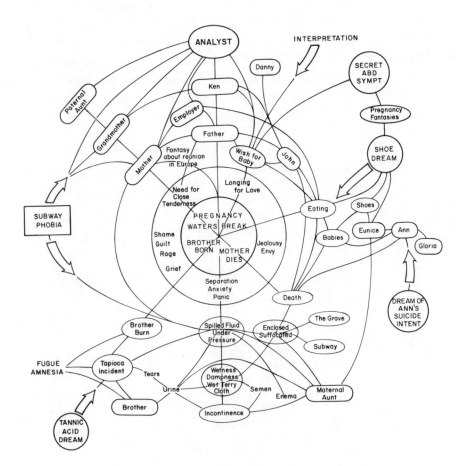

FIGURE 6.3

Carol's Enduring Nodal Memory Network

A series of cartoons (figures 6.3–6.8) depicts schematically (*not* literally) the enduring nodal memory network ("Mnet" scan) that can be constructed for Carol from the psychoanalytic process data recounted in chapters 4 and 5. Each of the "nodal points" and the connections among them represent actual verbal and imagery content that emerged and was talked about during the analytic hours. All of the connections and nodes in the psychoanalytic process data reported are summarized in figure 6.3. In figures 6.4–6.8, the total network appears behind an orienting shaded background, highlighting the specific connections that emerged during particular hours or in discussing particular events. Figure 6.4 depicts those that appeared in discussion of the tannic acid dream. Figure 6.5 depicts the network that lit up during the analysis of the subway phobia. Figures 6.6, 6.7, and 6.8 depict the connections that appeared in the three consecutive analytic hours reported in chapter 5. Figure 6.6 depicts the connections disclosed in the analysis of the dream of Ann's suicide intent. Figure 6.7 depicts the shoe dream—a response to the interpretation in the preceding hour of her wish for a baby. Figure 6.8 depicts the following hour—the analysis of the secret abdominal symptom.

tapioca incident and associative incidents link to the whole circuit or complex of nodal ideas, as well as to the brother's birth and the death of the mother and the breaking of the membranes. Figure 6.4 depicts how the tannic acid dream via the same linkages lit up that entire circuit of connections. Likewise, one can see (figure 6.5) how the subway phobia links up with many of the same connections.

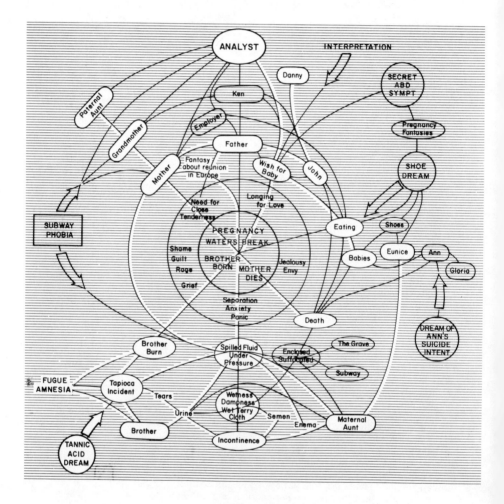

FIGURE 6.4
The Tannic Acid Dream

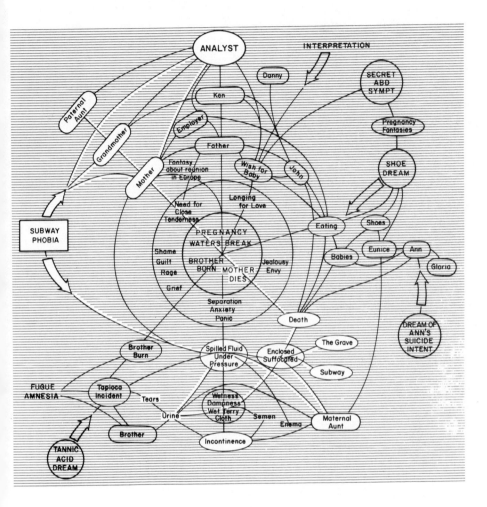

FIGURE 6.5
The Subway Phobia

The issues related to early life and childhood events are depicted on the lower part of this series of figures. They link up to current concerns through the issue of babies and pregnancy wishes, introduced by the dream of Ann's suicide intent (figure 6.6), which was followed by the shoe dream (figure 6.7) and, finally, the analysis of the secret symptom (figure 6.8).

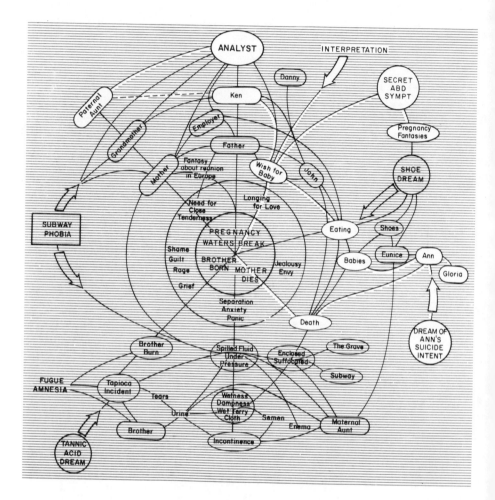

FIGURE 6.6
The Dream of Ann's Suicide Intent

The figures schematically depict a zone of affects surrounding the nuclear traumatic event like cytoplasm around the nucleus of the cell. Major affects are listed but the list is not meant to be complete, nor do affect zones traversed by the connecting lines specify links between affects and ideas. In most instances, the affective linkages will be clear in the reader's mind (the limitations of a two-dimensional scheme precluded

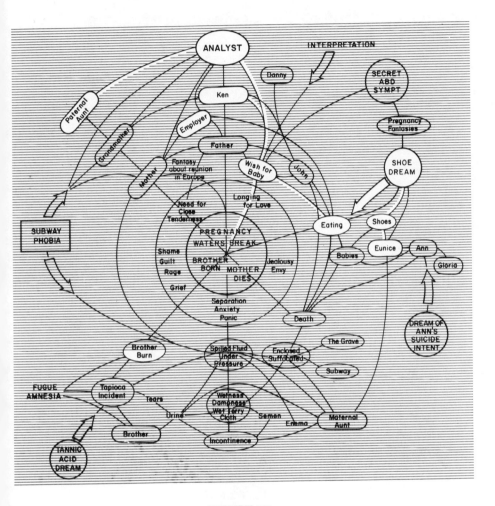

FIGURE 6.7
The Shoe Dream

trying to make those links go through specific affect zones).

The upper halves of the figures depict the important people in Carol's life and the ways in which wishes, needs, and strong feelings were directed to various ones of them, displaced from one to another, and so forth. They also clearly depict how when fully developed, the transference neurosis focused all of these currents onto the analyst.

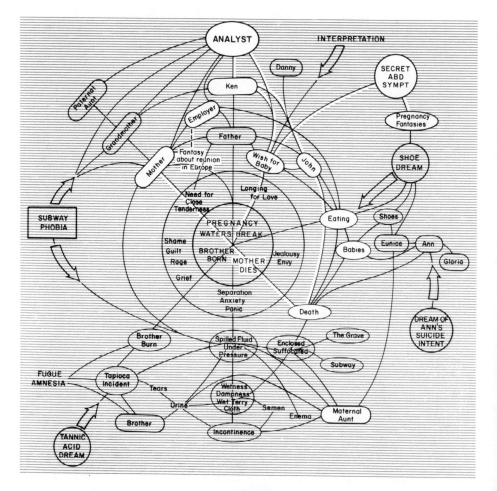

FIGURE 6.8
The Secret Abdominal Symptom

Closing Comments about Carol

As discussed more fully in chapter 3, the transference neurosis consists mainly of a vivid current revival of feelings and concerns that originated in crucial unresolved conflicts of childhood but that are experienced during analysis as current responses and feelings toward the analyst as a person. In every respect these feelings are felt by the patient to be real, currently alive, and belonging to the analyst. "Working through" can be thought of as dual processing—experiencing feelings as emotionally real and current while at the same time observing them cognitively as rooted in past conflicted relationships that can now be understood and resolved.

As you have probably already anticipated, Carol's feelings toward me were for a long time and for the most part dominated and shaped by what she had experienced with her father —and we have already seen how she defended against recognizing the forbidden erotic and pregnancy wishes by interposing Ken as a buffer. Note, though, that the threat of self-initiated, abrupt separation from Ken at the very start of our relationship revived the panic of the night of her mother's death, indicating that an aspect of the transferred feelings to Ken was rooted in dependent longings for Mother and that the transference neurosis included maternal as well as paternal aspects. The fact that Father had not wished to marry again as long as he had Carol—with the reverse implication that he would prefer for her not to marry—entered at the end into timing of termination. But that is getting ahead of the story.

Though Carol must have been exceptionally close to Father, she could not remember spending time with him before her brother was brought into the home—the only exceptions being the times she went with Father to visit her brother in the orphanage. Apparently, the intense feelings of gratification and guilt over having Father to herself during that epoch were too strong to persist in conscious memory. After Brother came to live with them, his continued bed-wetting forced the family to remove Carol from the bed where Brother slept to the studio couch in the living room. Each night, grandmother and aunts would retire and Father would sit reading in his easy chair at the head of the couch where Carol slept. When we first started to work, she was unwilling and unable to lie on the analytic couch until she remembered this situation. (This occurred after six months of work, and after that there was no problem about using the couch.) Many nights after Father retired to his bedroom, Carol would walk in her sleep and end up spending the rest of the night sleeping in Father's bed. For the first two-thirds of the analysis her appointment hours were at the end of the workday and my office was a twenty-five-minute bus ride uptown from her work. Each evening she would fall asleep on the bus but awaken promptly and regularly just before the correct stop for my office. Sound familiar? BUT one evening (when she had still felt drowsy in the waiting room) she said as she walked into the office, "When your office door opened signaling me to come in, it wasn't you I expected to see—I fully expected to see a pregnant woman!" (Mother again—riding piggyback, as it were, on the "father transference.")

At this point, I must supply an additional aspect of her medical history. She had suffered from "tic douloureux" since her early twenties, or for over ten years. It had come on following a local nerve block for a dental procedure. The attacks, which occurred two to three times a year, lasted several days, were incapacitating, and had been refractory to medical treatment measures.

In the third year of her analysis, I had to move to a location that would require over an hour's travel time for her each way. When I told her of the plan, I acknowledged the inconvenience it would entail and offered her the option of changing to a different analyst closer to her home and work. She jumped up, said, "God damn you," and without turning around ran out, slamming the door behind her. The next day she returned and reported that on hearing of the move she had felt the first twinges of a trigeminal neuralgic attack. The pain had mounted steadily for several hours, but so had her indignation and blinding rage. As the rage mounted, "the pain was swept away —as if it was dissolved by the flood of anger." That attack of trigeminal neuralgia stopped abruptly, and she did not have a fully developed attack in the ensuing seventeen years. Once every year or two, an attack would start. When it did, she would get angry at herself for getting it, and the anger seemed to abort the attack before it really developed. We never analyzed the meanings involved although we tried; we never recovered a forgotten incident. Was there one? We both "understand what happened," but the understanding is implicit and eludes words that would describe it.

The intensity of the response is reminiscent of the night Mother left her and of her search for Ken at the start of the analysis, but this time the *rage* is intense, conscious, and "up front." (What could the mechanism of this effect be?) She decided to continue working with me and here is a truly fascinating thing to ponder. It was not until I began to write the manuscript for this book that *I* realized that the subway line she was riding at the time she developed the subway phobia was the very same line (same station to board the train! same descent into the tunnel!) that she rode four times a week for the last year of analysis to come to my new office. Why did it take *me* so long (an additional thirteen years) to remember that fact? If you conclude that there must have been (be) some countertransference, what could I do but agree?

You will recall that the tannic acid dream was in the last year, at a point when the issue of termination had been raised but not settled. We decided that termination should not be contingent on her getting married, but could occur once we had worked through to as full an understanding as possible of the origin and nature of the conflicts that had blocked her from taking this step. We had also discussed the possibility that she might decide to marry but not have children. (Since she was by then thirty-nine years old, the outlook for pregnancy and childbirth was not optimistic, especially given her history and background.) This possibility was the one she eventually chose. She did take the European trip, without the fantasy reunion. She did not marry Danny—but fell in love and married satisfactorily a year after termination. You may have noticed that there has been an unusually long period of brief postanalytic contacts (the last one was five years ago for advice on a medical referral). At the last visit she expressed the thought that she had had to make sure from time to time that I was still alive and related this need to her fantasy that Mother must still be alive "somewhere else."

Well, that concludes the account. I have deliberately included clinical information that has been specifically discussed in the preceding chapters, and have intentionally left the memory network diagrams ("Mnet" scans) schematic and inexact. As mentioned earlier, these diagrams are not meant to be taken literally or in any exact sense. I am certain that many readers will have noted a large number of additional significant connections that I have not commented on or included in the discussion. It could go on and on. The question is whether the clinical process material conveys a sense of face validity. In any event, I hope it gives some idea of the richness and complexity of the process, of the analytic relationship, of the "analytic instrument," and of unanswered questions. "That's the way it is." Will an appreciation of where and how clinical psychoanalytic data are derived help with the central questions that motivated the writing of this book? Let's wait and see.

CHAPTER 7

Clarifying Terminology and Basic Concepts

IN preceding chapters I have tried using direct clinical data to describe and illustrate in detail what I regard to be essential features of the psychoanalytic process that render it a unique and powerful tool for the study of human mental processes, with memory functions serving as a specific case in point. Before proceeding further to issues to be confronted in the following sections of the book, I shall now go back and clarify as precisely as possible the sense in which I shall be using terms that refer to familiar psychoanalytic concepts. Such clarification is important for several reasons. First, because these terms may have somewhat different meanings when used by different authors, they are not always used in exactly the same ways. Second, I have throughout used descriptive and operational language in place of traditional psychoanalytic terminology wherever possible. Third, having decided to go back to "START," I have framed this discussion to underline and emphasize basic mechanisms and principles as first spelled out by Freud. Consequently, I neglect later additions and elaborations that would, of course, be important—even indispensable —in other contexts, but, I think, distracting in this one. For example, in this section of the book, terminology related to models of the mind, both topographic (Cs–Pcs–Ucs) and structural (id–ego–superego), has been for the most part deliberately omitted even in discussing such a critically important phenomenon as intrapsychic conflict. Clearly, such an omission would be serious in other contexts, in discussions meant to serve other goals and purposes than this one. (For a more complete introductory discussion see Brenner 1955.)

Accordingly, a disclaimer: what follows is not intended to be exhaustive or complete either in extent or in detail. I have tried to present those core concepts in psychoanalytic theory that seem to me germane to the focus of this book. And I have attempted to frame them in a form that could be elaborated on and added to in other contexts. There are five of them: instinct, the two principles of mental functioning (primary and secondary process thinking), repression, signal anxiety, and defenses.

Instinct

Instincts in psychoanalytic theory are regarded as innate (inborn) life processes manifest both bodily and mentally, as physicochemical and psychological phenomena. Instincts are thought to have their source in the (metabolic) life processes of tissue (cells) and to manifest themselves in the realm of the mind as motives, drives, or predispositions to behavior. Freud conceived the manifestation of an instinct in the mental sphere to be the measure of the demand for work placed on the mind by virtue of its connection with the body. (Perhaps the cerebrally directed arrows from organs to brain (cortex) in figure 13.2 could be taken to depict such an idea.) Instincts display three components: *source* (inflexible)—fixed in specific tissue processes (e.g., hormones); *aim*—consummating behavior (e.g., orgasm), which can be deflected (sexual intercourse, masturbation, et cetera); *object*—the person or thing that can satisfy the aim, quite a range of choices here (partner, erotic picture, et cetera). In other words, the source is invariant, the aim can be deflected within a wide range, and the target even more so, to encompass a wider variety of objects.

There are two paths whereby an instinct may impact on mental life: one via affect, the second via ideation. Ideational contents (e.g., images, thoughts, ideas, daydreams) stemming from instinctual sources are referred to as instinct derivatives. A wish is a prototypical example. Affective and ideational aspects of instinct derivatives are thought to be linked in the special and complicated ways in the associative mnemonic networks discussed in the preceding chapters.

Primary and Secondary Process Thinking

The realization that the mind simultaneously processes information in two fundamentally and radically different modes constitutes one of the most monumental of Freud's discoveries. The primary process, ontogenetically and phylogenetically older and more primitive (primary on two counts), proceeds largely but not entirely outside of consciousness in the awake adult but is easily observed in—even characteristic of—the conscious thinking of childhood (and adulthood in historically remote and less complex cultures). Secondary process is more familiar to us through our everyday introspection; it predominates in the conscious, deliberate, rational thinking of the mature adult. The two modes differ in respect both to type of thinking and to ways in which drive-motivated behaviors and affects appear to be modulated and regulated. The differences are manifested in respect to both the ideational and the affective aspects of the instinct.

Primary process thinking is strange and unfamiliar. It is characterized by its lack of logic, absence of a sense of time (timelessness), part representation for the whole, tolerance for mutually contradictory ideas to coexist or freely replace one another, absence of negatives, references by allusion, and predominance of the visual over the verbal mode to represent ideas. Freud discovered it in learning how to understand (decode) thoughts as expressed in dreams, parapraxes, and neurotic symptoms. Contrast this type of thought with secondary process thinking, which follows laws of logic and syntax and is deliberate, controlled, and predominantly verbal in representing ideas. In the primary process mode, controlled regulation of drive-motivated behavior and affects is highly inefficient or lacking altogether. Thus, frustration tolerance is low, there is little capacity to delay gratification, affects are manifest in powerful and intense form, and interest or attention can shift easily and "en masse" from one object to another (condensation and displacement). Behavior is impulsive and not guided strongly, if at all, by consideration of reality. In contrast, the secondary process mode is characterized by controlled modulated affects, high frustration tolerance, ability to delay gratification, relatively fixed and stable attention and interest, and behavior that is deliberate and carefully planned to conform with reality.

Very different principles are displayed in the way ideational and affective components of instincts relate to each other in the two modes of mental function. In primary process thought large amounts of affect are manifest and seem only very loosely connected with the corresponding ideational derivatives, as is observed in the mechanisms of condensation and displacement. In contrast, secondary process manifests smaller controlled displays of affect and tighter connection between affective and ideational components.

All of this suggested to Freud the operation of an underlying "energy" that not only drives the motor physiologic components of affect but also fuels thought processes. The primary process mode is considered to operate with large quantities of intense, highly mobile energies; the secondary process mode to operate with small, less intense, bound quantities. These ideas were later elaborated and developed by Hartmann (1958) in the concept of "neutralized, desexualized and de-aggressified energy."

Although these energy postulates remain controversial, I have introduced them to impart a reasonably good sense of the phenomena they were formulated to explain.

Freud himself to the end found the idea of psychic energy a baffling problem. In his last (posthumously published) work, *An Outline of Psycho-Analysis* (1940), he wrote:

> Here we have approached the still shrouded secret of the nature of the psychical. We assume, as other natural sciences have led us to expect, that in mental life some kind of energy is at work; but we have nothing to go upon which will enable us to come nearer to a knowledge of it by analogies with other forms of energy. We seem to recognize that nervous or psychical energy occurs in two forms, one freely mobile and another, by comparison, bound. . . . *Further than this we have not advanced* (pp. 163–64; italics added).

I do not consider it germane to the main purpose of this discussion (which is to convey an empirical understanding and appreciation of psychological phenomena that can be and are regularly observed as part of the psychoanalytic process) to decide or at this point to argue: (1) whether energy is actually involved and if so what its sources may be; (2) whether it is a reasonable and/or necessary hypothetical construct; and (3) whether the baby (psychoanalysis) should be thrown out with the bath water (hypothetical mental energy). Let's go on to the next core concept.

Repression

Repression refers to a special case of forgetting. The repressed is not merely or passively forgotten, that is, kept out of mind; it is considered to be actively kept out of mind in order to avoid intense psychic discomfort (affective arousal), which would ensue if it were to be recognized. How, according to the theory, is this accomplished? Freud hypothesized that an idea or thought can be consciously recognized as such (i.e., consciously apperceived, appreciated, and acknowledged) only when it can present with an explicit verbal label. Conversely, an identical ideational derivative will remain consciously unrecognized (unacknowledged or appreciated) when presented in a nonverbal (for example, visual) mode; thus, the message behind a charade or a rebus remains unrecognized until it can be rendered in words. At base, then, repression is considered to come about when an idea (along with its associated affectively charged memory traces) is somehow precluded from being explicitly labeled by words: its word representation is withdrawn and withheld, so to speak, and along with it the potential for activating associated affective components. Here one can see how the theory draws upon observational data. Consider the immense power of words in psychoanalytic process, exemplified by the interpretive power of a "switch" word to direct a patient's thought to an explicit connection between a specific word that he or she used (or could have used in referring to one idea) and a second idea that is in his or her mind but not consciously recognized and acknowledged. Recall my interpretation "You were spinning a daydream when the *delivery* man arrived." Carol was referring to the man *delivering* groceries. When she "caught on" that it also signified "obstetrician," the pregnancy-labor fantasy was "delivered"—pardon the pun—into consciousness.

Signal Anxiety

Anxiety occupies a position of central importance for understanding both physiologic and psychologic aspects of health and disease. Many of its physiologic manifestations are accessible both in humans and in animals to precise and detailed study in the experimental laboratory; likewise, many of its directly observable behavioral manifestations can be studied quantitatively as well as qualitatively in the experimental laboratory. Indeed, both of these approaches have shared happily in the exciting, almost unbelievable, pace of new discoveries and insights that has characterized work in the life sciences in recent years. Unhappily the same is not the case in respect to complex subjective intrapsychic aspects. For these, which are no less important, the psychoanalytic method—cumbersome, indirect, and far from ideal as it may be—is still the best available. It may even, if it can be properly harnessed, be capable of contributing (perhaps in modest but unique ways) to the mainstream advances that are occurring in the neurosciences.

First, let us get back to the task at hand and review the basic elements of the psychoanalytic theory of anxiety. The theory starts with the assumption that each human being begins life with an innate capacity for the combined physiologic-psychologic response we call anxiety—more about the phenomenon itself later (chapters 9, 10, 11, 12, and 13). The theory emphasizes the distinction between fear, in which the danger stimulus is external and recognized, and anxiety, in which the danger stimulus is internal and unrecognized. Thus, anxiety may occur when there is a conflict between an unconscious wish and the person's opposing mature goals and moral standards. External threat can be dealt with by "fight or flight." Since neither option is possible when the danger is internal, the psychological defenses had to be developed in mental life as equivalent mechanisms for dealing with internal threat. The defenses are thought to be cued into action by an attenuated (subclinical) anxiety reaction that occurs when an unconscious conflicted wish threatens to achieve recognition in consciousness and access to the motor apparatus. Such a wish, if unopposed and put into action, could, in fact, eventuate in real danger (for example, murder of a parent would result in irreplaceable loss of a loved and needed person and/or in severe punishment).

Freud conceived the attenuated anxiety reaction to have been developed in the course of evolution as an *adaptive signal* of impending danger—a signal that would, in turn, activate reactive measures (defenses) that could oppose or block the primitive instinctual derivative from achieving consciousness and motor expression. He postulated "signal anxiety" to be an attenuated version of a primitive and powerful total organismic response ("automatic anxiety") to intense, pervasive, and overpowering external and internal stimulations. He labeled such a situation a "traumatic situation" and offered as the prototype the circumstances of birth—the initial major separation experience for the human being. Because of the far-reaching implications of these concepts, which have been so thoroughly incorporated into clinical psychiatric theory as to have rendered their origin obscure, even forgotten, here I will quote at unusual length from the pri ary source in order that the reader may have firsthand exposure to the full dimension and style of Freud's thinking.

If the structure and origin of anxiety are as described, the next question is: what is the function of anxiety and on what occasions is it reproduced? The answer seems to be obvious and convincing: anxiety arose originally as a reaction to a state of *danger* and it is reproduced whenever a state of that kind recurs.
This answer, however, raises further considerations. The innervations involved in the original state of anxiety probably had a meaning and purpose, in just the same way as the muscular movements which accompany a first hysterical attack. . . . Thus at birth it is probable that the innervation, in being directed to the respiratory organs, is preparing the way for the activity of the lungs, and, in accelerating the heartbeat, is helping to keep the blood free from toxic substances. Naturally, when the anxiety-state is reproduced later as an affect it will be lacking in any such expediency, just as are the repetitions of a hysterical attack. When the individual is placed in a new situation of danger it may well be quite inexpedient for him to respond with an anxiety-state (which is a reaction to an earlier danger) instead of initiating a reaction appropriate to the current danger. *But his behaviour may become expedient once more if the danger-situation is recognized as it approaches and is signalled by an outbreak of anxiety.* . . . Thus we see that there are two ways in which anxiety can emerge: in an inexpedient way, when a new situation of danger has occurred, or in an expedient way . . . in order to give a signal and prevent such a situation from occurring (Freud 1926, pp. 134–35; italics added).

Freud then goes on to delineate the "danger situations."

Only a few of the manifestations of anxiety in children are comprehensible to us, and we must confine our attention to them. They occur, for instance, when a child is alone, or in the dark, or when it finds itself with an unknown person instead of one to whom it is used—such as its mother. These three instances can be reduced to a single condition—namely, that of missing someone who is loved and longed for. But here, I think, we have the key to an understanding of anxiety and to a reconciliation of the contradictions that seem to beset it. . . .

This anxiety has all the appearance of being an expression of the child's feeling at its wits' end, as though in its still very undeveloped state it did not know how better to cope with its cathexis of longing. *Here anxiety appears as a reaction to the felt loss of the object;* and we are at once reminded of the fact that castration anxiety, too, is a fear of being separated from a highly valued object, and that *the earliest anxiety of all—the 'primal anxiety' of birth—is brought about on the occasion of a separation from the mother.*

But a moment's reflection takes us beyond this question of loss of object. The reason why the infant in arms wants to perceive the presence of its mother is only because it already knows by experience that she satisfies all its needs without delay. The situation, then, which it regards as a 'danger' and against which it wants to be safeguarded is that of non-satisfaction, of a *growing tension due to need,* against which it is helpless. I think that if we adopt this view all the facts fall into place. The situation of non-satisfaction in which the amounts of stimulation rise to an unpleasurable height without its being possible for them to be mastered psychically or discharged must for the infant be analogous to the experience of being born—must be a repetition of the situation of danger. What both situations have in common is the economic disturbance caused by an accumulation of amounts of stimulation which require to be disposed of. It is this factor, then, which is the real essence of 'danger'. In both cases the reaction of anxiety sets in. (This reaction is still an expedient one in the infant in arms, for the discharge, being directed into the respiratory and vocal muscular apparatus, now calls its mother to it, just as it activated the lungs of the new-born baby to get rid of the internal stimuli.) . . .

When the infant has found out by experience that an external, perceptible object can put an end to the dangerous situation which is reminiscent of birth, the content of the danger it fears is displaced from the economic situation on to the condition which determined that situation, viz., the loss of object. *It is the absence of the mother that is now the danger;* and as soon as that danger arises the infant gives the signal of anxiety, before the dreaded economic situation has set in. *This change constitutes a first great step forward in the provision made by the infant for its self-preservation, and at the same time represents a transition from the automatic and involuntary fresh appearance of anxiety to the intentional reproduction of anxiety as a signal of danger.*

In these two aspects, as an automatic phenomenon and as a rescuing signal, anxiety is seen to be a product of the infant's mental helplessness which is a natural counterpart of its biological helplessness. The striking coincidence by which the anxiety of the new-born baby and the anxiety of the infant in arms are both conditioned by separation from the mother does not need to be explained on psychological lines. It can be accounted for simply enough biologically; for, just as the mother originally satisfied all the needs of the foetus through the apparatus of her own body, so now, after its birth, she continues to do so, though partly by other means. There is much more continuity between intra-uterine life and earliest infancy than the impressive caesura of the act of birth would have us believe. What happens is that the child's biological situation as a foetus is replaced for it by a psychical object-relation to its mother. . . .

The significance of the loss of object as a determinant of anxiety extends considerably further. For the next transformation of anxiety, viz. the castration anxiety belonging to the phallic phase, is also a fear of separation and is thus attached to the same determinant. In this case the danger is of being separated from one's genitals. . . .

The progress which the child makes in its development—its growing independence, the sharper division of its mental apparatus into several agencies, the advent of new needs—cannot fail to exert an influence upon the content of the danger-situation. We have already traced the change of that content from loss of the mother as an object to castration. The next change is caused by the power of the super-ego. With the depersonalization of the parental agency from which castration was feared, the danger becomes less defined. Castration anxiety develops into moral anxiety—social anxiety—and it is not so easy now to know what the anxiety is about. The formula, 'separation and expulsion from the horde', only applies to that later portion of the super-ego which has been formed on the basis of social prototypes, not to the nucleus of the super-ego, which corresponds to the introjected parental agency. Putting it more generally, what the ego regards as the danger and responds to with an anxiety-signal is that the super-ego should be angry with it or punish it or cease to love it. The final transformation which the fear of the super-ego undergoes is, it seems to me, the fear of death (or fear for life) which is a fear of the super-ego projected on to the powers of destiny (Freud 1926, pp. 136–40; italics added).

Forbidden conflicted impulses, if unopposed, would lead to danger situations, the nature of which changes as the child grows older: for the infant, the loss of the mother's presence; later, loss of mother's love, castration; and finally, in the older child, guilt—disapproval and punishment by the superego. "Danger situations" are regarded as ones that portend development of a "traumatic situation" and automatic anxiety unless (defensive) steps (initiated by generation of signal anxiety) are taken to avert it. These ideas are further discussed in chapter 11, in relation to biological data and adaptive evolutionary considerations.

The Psychological Defense Mechanisms

The psychological defenses, then, are conceptualized as unconscious mental mechanisms that block or prevent explicit conscious recognition of ideational derivatives of forbidden or conflicted instinctual motives and thereby block access to the motor systems. Anna Freud (1946) regards repression as the first-line defense backed up by a host of others, most of which in this theoretical context can be thought of as exploiting the vicissitudes of the instincts (i.e., the capacity of the instinctual aims to be modified and deflected onto a wide range of substitute objects). Meissner (1980), following Vaillant (1971), classifies defense mechanisms as narcissistic, immature, neurotic, and mature. Leigh and I (1982) have proposed a taxonomy based on general systems concepts (Miller 1978). In other words, as is shown in table 7.1, the taxonomy is organized around the functional personality subsystems primarily involved: (1) those affecting input systems (perception); (2) those affecting internal processing systems (cognitive and affective processes); (3) those affecting output systems (action); and (4) those affecting all subsystems evenly by affecting the executive function (Leigh and Reiser 1982). The advantages of this classification system (to anticipate ideas to come in the next

TABLE 7.1

Classification of Defense Mechanisms

The Input Subsystem	*The Output Subsystem*
Denial	Counterphobic maneuvers
Displacement	Undoing
Projection	Sublimation
Introjection	Activity and acting out
Constriction of awareness	Withdrawal and avoidance
Internal Processing Subsystem	*The "Decider" or "Executive" Subsystem*
Repression	Regression
Rationalization	Identification
Intellectualization	
Isolation	
Fantasy and daydreaming	
Reaction formation	

SOURCE: A version of this table appeared in H. Leigh and M. F. Reiser, "A general systems taxonomy for psychological defense mechanisms," *Journal of Psychosomatic Research* 26 (1982): 80–81. Reprinted with permission of Hoyle Leigh and Pergamon Press, Ltd.

chapter) are that it relates primarily to directly observable phenomena that can be readily classified and that it may generate researchable neuropsychologic hypotheses concerning possible neural substrata of defense mechanisms.

CHAPTER 8

Where Do We Go
from Here?

THERE are two directions that seem to me worth considering. The first derives from a point already made that I want to reemphasize and extend here. It is that the psychoanalytic process provides an immensely powerful method for the study of human memory function—one with perhaps unique potential for uncovering important relationships between cognitive and affective aspects. This is because of the power of the psychoanalytic process to recover memory traces, perceptual registrations that have been stored but have been forgotten and have remained forgotten—presumably to avoid anticipated intolerable affective distress. But I hasten to add again that its power is matched by the extent to which it is unwieldy, at least within the constraints of conventional methods of natural science. Because its data cannot be consensually validated, because its observations cannot be replicated or pass criteria of reliability, they are unfortunately lost to the public domain of the behavioral and neural sciences.

Still there must be—and I am convinced there are—ways to enlist (entrain, if you will) its potential power into the mainstream of behavioral and neurobiologic-neuroscience research endeavors.

The First Direction: Generating Questions from Process Data

Consider again, if you will, the discussion of Carol's memory network with its nodal points and core nuclear conflicts. This memory network very clearly provided links for understanding major and minor symptoms (phobias for marriage, for pregnancy, later for the subway; the hysterical dissociated state with fugue and amnesia) and for understanding symptomatic behaviors and character traits (e.g., the defensive acting-out relationship with Ken, the guilty, anger-provoking pattern of relating to men, her "thing" about damp towels). You will recall also how this core network progressively unfolded—or, to put it another way, was retraced bit by bit—as the analytic process progressed. Frequently a dream would lead us into it, as occurred with the shoe dream (figure 6.7), which followed an interpretation that confronted her defenses against the previously unrecognized wish to have a baby and was followed by understanding of a "secret" symptom that clearly expressed that wish in disguised form (figure 6.8). Much later the path to the same core conflict was traced via work on another dream (figure 6.4), which led to recovery of the amnesia from the dissociated fugue state and in turn, via common (nodal point) links, to remembering childhood incidents (the enema) and, finally, to events connected with her mother's pregnancy, labor, and death and her own guilty preoccupation with these events. Much later still it was reentered again when we analyzed the subway phobia (figure 6.5) that developed many years after the analysis.

Consider, too, how all elements in the memory network led

ultimately to the transference neurosis, which provided the vehicle for "working through" the nuclear conflict. In this context, remember, if you will, how essential *remembering* the historical (analogous and homologous) experiences was for gaining an intellectual understanding and perspective *while* (re)experiencing the affects. Is the reexperiencing of the affect sometimes the first (vanguard) form of remembering the event? (Often it seems to be.) Recall the almost mysterious memory phenomena that occurred in the analyst and the questions they generate concerning empathy and countertransference (implicating affective and cognitive interactions) as well as concerning the state of mind in which "the analytic instrument" seems to work best.

Clearly the analytic process has the power to generate a myriad of intriguing questions. But can these questions be put to use? Do they have any heuristic value? "Not unless they are testable," you will say and you will be right. Now here we come to a crucially important issue. Can the raw data of the clinical psychoanalytic process directly or even indirectly generate questions that can be investigated within the psychoanalytic context or within the context of other disciplines by investigators using more conventional experimental and statistical methods? Is it possible that following such a strategy could even lead to generation of testable hypotheses—testable in model experimental systems?

Let's backtrack a little historically. The idea that psychoanalytic theory could be tested productively in conventional experimental settings surely is a sound one and it is not new. But many earlier efforts dealt with attempts to validate abstract hypotheses derived from metapsychological theory. Whereas such hypotheses had the advantage of being cast in experimentally testable form, often this was achieved at the expense of trivializing issues—of leading to experiments that did not constitute tests of clinically meaningful hypotheses, even if the data met criteria of reliability.

What I want to suggest that *is* new is really old, namely, that we go to START—back to the "intellectual set," if you will, that Freud held in response to his direct clinical observations when he so confidently expected the sciences of the brain to furnish the answers. In his time he was disappointed and gave up his "Project for a Scientific Psychology" (Freud 1895), instead focusing exclusively on psychological methods of study. Freud made this shift, I think, not only because he preferred psychological methods, or for other reasons, but also and mainly because knowledge of nervous system function was then so incomplete—so crude, in fact, as to preclude using the term "neuroscience" in its current sense to refer to it.

But think how different it is today! It does now seem feasible to develop philosophically appropriate and empirically sound conceptual bridges between modern neuroscience and psychoanalysis. I am proposing that it will be worthwhile for this purpose to develop new methods and strategies for approaching clinical data.

Hypotheses derived from metapsychological theory are not only many steps removed from the rich empirical data of clinical process but also, having been derived from metaphorical abstractions, are isolated from articulation with the concepts and data of the natural sciences. Hypotheses derived more directly from clinical process should have greater potential for being experimentally testable in the laboratories of basic neurobiologic scientists.

Referring to those abstract hypotheses derived from metapsychological theory, Kubie expressed similar ideas in 1952:

... my fear is of allowing a subtle, anthropomorphizing tendency to inflate these abstractions from the whole personality, endowing each with a spurious independent existence, which then would allow us to indulge ourselves in allegorical imagery and figures of speech. ... These are conceptual and terminological naivetés and confusions which must be simplified and clarified by analysts themselves before we have a right to appeal to the experimental scientist for help with them (p. 105).

But I do not mean to suggest that experimentally testable hypotheses can be extracted immediately from raw clinical data such as I have presented here. However I *am* suggesting that it may be worthwhile to focus on the analytic process itself and the questions it can generate about specific aspects of mental function. Some preliminary steps need to be taken in processing the data. The first (and most important) step would already have taken place within the mind of the analyst, which all the time is reducing, sorting, and organizing the data, albeit largely outside the conscious focus of his attention. Even though the final "printout" in consciousness is not subject to consensual validation in the ordinary sense, we probably ought not throw it away. Instead, it could go through the next step of usual scientific process; that is, it could be put through the "filter" of preliminary logical and experiential criteria to determine whether it seems reasonable to regard it as a promising "crude ore."

1. Do the clinical formulations of the analyst have face validity?
2. Are they internally consistent and logical? Do others experienced in the use of psychoanalytic method recognize them as familiar, feasible, consistent with their "impressions" from work with other patients?
3. Can their relation to their empirical base be explicated?
4. Clinically, do they have explanatory power?
5. Do the derivative issues they raise have the potential to be focused (on a specific aspect of, say, memory or anxiety) and cast in the form of reasonable questions to be directed to appropriate antidisciplines?

I raised as samples some first tentative questions of this last sort (criterion 5 above) in recounting and discussing the work with Carol. They were broad and general questions (from "parent discipline" to "antidiscipline"). Some of them were:

1. *Where* in the brain and *how* had that memory trace been stored for twenty-five years?
2. Why and how did it come to be remembered?
3. What is the nature of the processes that make such motivated forgetting and remembering possible?

Criteria 1–4 pertain to the clinical data that gave rise to the questions just posed. I hope most clinicians and readers would agree that the observations and clinical formulations would pass the screen of the direct criteria 1–4. The issues or questions I have listed (and it would be possible to conjure up many more, and in fact, others were included in chapters 4 and 5) are more challenging. And it seems to me that these questions do have potential to focus on specific aspects of memory in forms appropriate for consideration by other disciplines. In fact, these are the questions that guided the selection of neurobiologic studies to be reviewed and discussed in part III.

The Second Direction: Rethinking Clinical Psychoanalytic Theory

A second direction that I envision as promising is closely related to the first. It evolves from the same principles as the first and departs only slightly from it. This direction also is not new; rather, it seems to have been forgotten and/or mistakenly neglected. What I propose is rethinking clinical psychoanalytic theory and attempting to recast at least some of that theory into forms that emphasize and are consonant with its empirical base and into forms that resemble conceptual and phenomenological patterns that have been and are currently useful in the biological sciences, thereby facilitating articulation with them. It should be feasible to accomplish such a task without introducing distortions or fundamental changes in essentials of the theory if we stick close to the observational data. After all, the empirical data stay the same no matter what we say or how we say it.

The classification scheme for psychological defenses proposed at the close of chapter 7 may serve as a first example. I will pursue several additional and more exciting examples at length and in greater detail in part III.

Finally, in closing this part of the book, I should add that as

Where Do We Go from Here?

Edelson (1983, 1984) has pointed out and as Luborsky (1973) has demonstrated, it is possible to develop hypotheses that can be tested within the psychoanalytic situation itself. The crucible of the psychoanalytic method should be capable of extracting increasingly refined material from the crude ore and supplying more readily researchable questions for biology.

Part III

BRAIN

THE

NEUROBIOLOGIC

SIDE

CHAPTER 9

How May Nerve Cells "Remember"?

THE FIRST "answering data" from neurobiology will come from studies that may seem surprisingly distant from the issues we've been considering so far. To address these studies properly, I must ask the reader to clear his circuits and take up a new position—a position that is on the other side and at the other end of the one from which we have been approaching the intermediate conceptual template described in chapter 1. But the transition, however abrupt it may seem, will provide a vivid and rewarding experience. It will consist of looking at an elegant, critically important, and exciting programmatic series of studies that answers questions we would not even have dared to ask as recently as twenty years ago—there would have been no way to answer them. And this series of studies promises to continue raising and answering new questions of which we have not yet even dreamed. I am referring to the neurophysiologic and cell biological approach to the study of behavior in relatively simple animal model systems.

The Neurobiologic Approach

The neurobiologic approach to the study of behavior involves the work of a great many investigators. I will focus primarily on the programmatic research of Eric Kandel and his colleagues. Their work on the marine snail *Aplysia* occupies a leading position in the field and is especially germane to the issues I am attempting to engage in this book. To set the background properly, I feel it is important to have Kandel's own words, that is, to quote rather than paraphrase his statement of the logical, philosophical bases and rationale for this uniquely important and significant research.

Although new in its application to behavior, a reductionist approach based upon the selection of technically congenial systems is traditional within biology. Advances have routinely depended on the selection and development of suitably simple experimental systems in which a family of interrelated problems can be studied effectively.

When it comes to behavior, however, one has somehow been reluctant to apply a reductionist's strategy. It is often said that behavior is the one area in biology in which simple animal models, particularly invertebrate ones, are least likely to be successful. The organization of the mammalian brain, and in particular the brain of man, is so complex that a comparative and reductionist approach to behavior based upon a study of invertebrates is bound to fail. Man has intellectual capabilities, language and abstract thinking, that are not found among simpler animals and that require types of neuronal organization qualitatively different from those found in invertebrates. Although these arguments are, in part, correct, they overlook certain critical issues. The issue is not whether there is something special about the human brain. There clearly is. The issue is rather whether the human brain and human behavior have *anything at all in common* with the brain and the behavior of simpler animals. If there are points of similarity, these might indicate that common principles of organization are involved, principles that could profitably be studied in simple animals.

The answer to the question of similarity is clear. Detailed work by students of comparative behavior such as Konrad Lorenz (1965), Niko Tinbergen (1951) and Karl von Frisch (1950) has shown that man shares many common behavioral patterns with simple animals, including elementary perception, motor coordination, and simple forms of learning. These findings, of course, do not guarantee that common neuronal mechanisms are actually involved in comparable aspects of behavior or learning in invertebrates and vertebrates, but the findings are encouraging and suggest that aspects of common mechanisms are likely to be involved. That the evolution of behavior is conservative should not be surprising. The evolution of other biological functions is similarly conservative. To choose a comparison that readily comes to mind, there are no fundamental functional or biochemical differences between the nerve cells and synapses of man and those of a snail. *Since behavior is a reflection of nerve cell activity, it is perhaps not surprising that the behavior of man has at least some elementary features in common with that of the snail. For in the neuronal mechanisms of behavior, as in other areas of biology, similar solutions are likely to be found again and again throughout phylogeny* (italics added). As a result, one is encouraged to think that a complete and rigorous analysis of behavior and learning in an invertebrate, no matter how simple the animal or the task, is likely to reveal mechanisms that will be of general importance. This rationale has provided the logical and philosophical basis for the current interest in the cellular mechanisms of behavior and learning in invertebrates (Kandel 1978, pp. 4–5).

Therein lies the importance of this invertebrate research to the task at hand. It seems eminently reasonable to me to expect that basic mechanisms found in simple systems are apt to be utilized as basic modules in higher forms. They could well be elaborated and/or combined into more complex arrays in order to subserve the far more complex functions required in higher species such as man. If that is true, clarification of their organizing principles should make it easier in the long run to understand the complexities of the brain and of the mind of humans. The work to be reviewed relates to the questions raised earlier from the parent discipline: *How* may memory traces be stored and how may they be remembered?

The Nervous System and Behavior: Basic Principles

First, let me quickly review some basic, generally accepted organizational and functional principles about the nervous system and behavior. Neurobiologic studies have shown that it is interaction between nerve cells that mediates behavior. Nerve cells are interconnected in specific ways. An organism's behavioral potential is genetically encoded as specificity of the wiring that will develop within its nervous system. Neurons communicate with each other mainly by releasing neurotransmitter substances at their synapses, enabling them to send on information rapidly through point-to-point contact. Not only the wiring of the neuronal networks but also the mechanisms governing synthesis and release of neurotransmitter substances are encoded in the genes. But it is highly important to note that learning and experience also can and do influence behaviors and the ultimate potential for behavior. They do these things by affecting the strength of synaptic transmission. The experiential effects on strength of synaptic function are powerful and profound in that they are capable of producing long-lasting changes in behavior. They are also developmentally important. Proper structural and functional development of the nervous system may depend on the presence of appropriate stimuli and experiences during "critical periods" of ontogeny. Even structural changes in transmitter regions of the synaptic nerve terminals may be induced by learning and experience. It is neuronal networks, then, that mediate behavior. The presence of, absence of, and the patterning of emergent behavior ultimately depend on strength of specific transsynaptic communication between the individual neurons that make up subsets and systems of the overall network.

Learning in *Aplysia*

Aplysia californica, a giant marine snail, often growing to a length of 30 cm and a weight of 1 kg, has provided an exemplary animal model system for study by combined behavioral, neurophysiologic, and cell biologic methods. Its behavioral repertoire is limited and its nervous system is numerically simple (approximately 20,000 central neurons clustered in nine groups of ganglia containing about 2,000 cells each). The nerve cell bodies cluster around the periphery of the ganglia (they can be visualized readily), and they are large. It is therefore possible accurately to record most synaptic and other threshold potentials generated in the axons and dendrites in the neuropil in the neuronal cell bodies. There is another feature that makes them especially amenable to study: the same neuron can be identified repeatedly in different individuals, and so the neuron can be named and the connections and interconnections between cells mapped, thereby making it possible to work out the wiring diagram of given behaviors.

In his Grass Lecture at the Seventh Annual Meeting of the Society for Neuroscience, Eric Kandel (1978) summarized three ideas emerging from key findings that he and his colleagues working with *Aplysia,* and other investigators working with various other invertebrates, had obtained up to that time:

1. Many neurons of a brain are unique individuals that make highly specific connections with other neurons or effector organs.
2. Individual cells have specific and often unique roles in behavior.
3. Certain types of learning result from changes in the activity of specific cells and from changes in the connections between cells.

It is important to specify the sense in which the term "learning" is used in this work; it is used in a broad sense, referring to modification of behavior as a result of exposure to a stimulus —whether or not that stimulus is associated with other stimuli or responses. "Memory, then, is the persistence of the learned modification—its storage, maintenance, and retrieval at various times after the completion of the learning task" (Kandel 1978). In the sense of this explicit operational definition, learning encompasses a hierarchy of behavioral modifications, from simple nonassociative forms such as habituation, dishabituation, and sensitization to more complex associative forms of learning such as classical and instrumental conditioning. The behaviors studied in *Aplysia* now extend upward to include associative learning in the form of classical conditioning. It should be noted, however, that the operational definition given here refers to the remembering or repetition of behaviors, which is not the same as the remembering of complex perceptually registered memory traces, or "engrams," connected with previously forgotten experiences, the type of remembering usually addressed in human (cognitive) psychology.

It will be worthwhile, I think, to follow the story as it unfolds, starting with habituation—"the decrease in behavioral response that occurs when an initially novel stimulus is repeatedly presented" (Kandel 1978). Habituation is the way organisms, including humans, learn to ignore stimuli that have lost meaning or novelty, and it serves an important and necessary adaptive function. Retention can be regarded as a measure of memory in this type of learning.

Habituation in *Aplysia* can be demonstrated by the siphon and gill withdrawal reflex. The respiratory organ of *Aplysia*— the gill—is housed in the mantle cavity, which is covered by the mantle shelf, a protective sheet that terminates in a fleshy spout—the siphon. When a weak or moderately intense tactile stimulus is applied either to the mantle shelf or the siphon, both the siphon and the gill contract into the mantle cavity. This reflex can undergo both habituation and sensitization.

Sensitization is more complex. It resembles classical conditioning in that activity in one pathway facilitates reflex activity in another but, unlike classical conditioning, does not require specific temporal association. It is a process in which an animal learns to increase a given reflex as a result of a noxious novel stimulus. Memory for both habituation and sensitization can be short-term or long-term depending on the pattern of stimulation. A special example of sensitization, dishabituation (the enhancement of a habituated response by a strong stimulus), was studied in *Aplysia* by applying a noxious mechanical or electrical stimulus to the head or neck of an animal in which the gill withdrawal had just been habituated. This resulted in facilitating or restoring the response.

The neuronal circuitry was demonstrated—and it is relatively simple (only one to five synapses are involved). And the cell biological analysis of both habituation and sensitization extends to the molecular biological level, including detailed fine structural study of the morphological changes that can be demonstrated by electron microscopy to occur in the sensory varicosities of the involved synapses (Bailey and Chen 1983). The long-term learning experience actually leads, then, to structural change within the cell!

The experimental findings to be discussed in the passages that follow were obtained by studying synaptic transmission between, and the electrical responsivity of, identified individual neurons of the gill withdrawal neuronal circuits of animals that demonstrated habituation, sensitization, or classical conditioning after exposure to appropriate experimental protocols. Similar cellular preparations were utilized also to study the effects of substances such as serotonin and cyclic AMP on synaptic transmission, and in the experimental analysis of chemical and molecular changes occurring in the neurons under study.

The critical functional changes occur at the excitatory chemical synapses that the sensory neurons make with the motor neurons. In habituation, with repeated stimulation, the sensory neuron terminals release progressively less neurotransmitter at the synaptic junction.[1] In sensitization, neurotransmission at the synapses of the sensory neurons on their target cells is altered by the mechanism of presynaptic facilitation. Facilitating interneurons, which are thought to be serotonergic, end on the terminals of sensory neurons and facilitate their ability to release neurotransmitter.[2]

To demonstrate classical conditioning in *Aplysia*, a chemical stimulus—crude shrimp extract—was used as the neutral conditioned stimulus. Since *Aplysia* is an herbivore and normally ignores shrimp, the extract, which is an effective chemical signal, can be used as an effective neutral stimulus (CS). The unconditioned stimulus was a shock to the head. The conditioned reflex was escape locomotion and other defensive reflexes in response to a weak test electric shock to the tail. The cellular mechanisms underlying classical conditioning in *Aplysia* have been shown to be related to those of long-term sensitization (see below). (The animal's or organism's response to the noxious stimulus (US) and then to the conditioned stimulus (CS) has been conceptualized by Kandel as a "learned motivational state" that can be regarded as a form of anxiety. This model paradigm, then, can be utilized in the study of anxiety as well as memory.)

The analytic steps thus far demonstrate:

1. That long-term habituation leads to prolonged and profound functional inactivation of a previously existing connection—that is, long-term change in synaptic efficiency can underlie a specific instance of long-term memory. The mechanism involves decrease in neurotransmitter release at the synaptic terminal of the sensory neuron.

2. That sensitization also alters neurotransmission at the same sensory terminals on target motor cells but in the opposite direction from habituation, that is, by increasing neurotransmitter release through the activity of serotonergic facilitating interneurons. Serotonin acting on a receptor sets up a biochemical cascade within the presynaptic terminals of the sensory cell which eventuates in molecular changes and enhanced neurotransmission.[3]

3. Classical conditioning involves a modified (augmented) form of presynaptic facilitation utilizing the same cellular and molecular mechanisms that underlie sensitization. This modified form, called *activity-dependent enhancement of presynaptic facilitation,* results from activation of serotonergic cells in the head ganglia that are part of the conditioned stimulus pathways. This activation in turn renders the sensory neuron terminals more responsive to the serotonin that has been released by other neurons, namely the facilitating interneurons of the unconditioned stimulus pathway (the same ones involved in sensitization of the gill withdrawal reflex).

Thus classical conditioning uses an application of the molecular mechanism used by sensitization, suggesting that there may be a molecular alphabet to learning whereby complex forms of learning use components found in simple forms. In signalled anxiety these presynaptic facilitating mechanisms appear to be used for two components of the learning at two points in the neural circuit: an associative component to provide for the temporal specifics of the modulation and a modulating component to enhance defensive activities (Kandel 1983, p. 1290).

Kandel (1983, p. 1291) finally concludes, "Thus, these studies suggest that there is a basic molecular grammar underlying the various forms of anxiety, a set of mechanistic building blocks that can be used in different combinations and permutations. They further suggest that a variety of mental processes that appear phenotypically unrelated may share a fundamental unity on the cellular and molecular levels."

No anatomic rearrangement in the nervous system is involved—neurons and synapses are neither created nor destroyed. What is involved in learning of habituation, sensitization, and classical Pavlovian conditioning are *changes in the functional effectiveness of previously existing chemical synaptic terminals* via modulation of calcium influx in the presynaptic terminals. All of this is effected in complex genetically determined pathways by learning and experience!

Extension to Mammalian Models

Many of the basic neurophysiologic principles developed in the invertebrate studies just described can also be observed to obtain in more complex mammalian models. (Findings from the latter have even led to ultimate *clinical* application in the human.) Over a period of many years, Michael Davis and his colleagues at Yale have pursued a carefully detailed and technically sophisticated programmatic series of psychophysiologic, neuroanatomic, neurophysiologic, and neuropharmacologic studies of the startle reflex in the rat (Davis 1980).

This reflex, occurring in a higher species—and therefore accessible to more advanced behavioral analysis—shares the advantages of relatively simple neuronal circuitry (its latency is 8 milliseconds, indicating that only a few central synapses are involved; and most details of the circuitry have already been worked out by Davis and his group). In addition, the startle reflex is sensitive to a variety of experimental situations. It is under stimulus control; it demonstrates habituation, sensitization, and modification by prior associative learning; it is sensitive to a variety of drugs and is currently being used to analyze how drugs alter sensorimotor reactivity. Centrally active biogenic amines play a part in mediating and influencing the reflex. Serotonin, for example, has a complex effect: in the forebrain it is inhibitory, in the spinal cord it exerts an excitatory effect. Dopamine and norepinephrine also are involved —in different ways. A wide variety of drug effects have been studied. When the reflex has been potentiated in the presence of a cue that has been previously paired with shock, it may be decreased by drugs that reduce anxiety in humans (e.g., alcohol, diazepam, sodium amytal, flurazepam, morphine, clonidine, and propranolol).

Results from the study of the startle reflex in the rat have already been shown to generalize to different stimulus-response systems in other species, including humans (Davis, in press). Potentialities for application in humans should be apparent. In chapter 12, we shall see in detail how the principles and theoretical explanations derived from data in these simple systems have actually extended progressively "upward"— from studies of single neurons to intermediate rodent and non-human primate systems and, finally, to the human, where clinical applications have even been found.

NOTES

1. This results from prolonged decrease of calcium influx, which in turn reflects the fact that repeated action potentials in the terminals decrease the number of open

How May Nerve Cells "Remember"?

Ca^{++} channels in the sensory terminal. Ca^{++} is thought to be required for the vesicles of neurotransmitter to bind to release sites.

2. The facilitating interneurons are thought to release serotonin, which is responsible for increasing the availability of Ca^{++} channels by acting on an adenylate cyclase in sensory neuron terminals, stimulating the synthesis of cyclic AMP within the cell. This in turn increases availability of Ca^{++} channels and leads to increased calcium influx and greater binding of vesicles of neurotransmitter to release sites.

3. Klein and Kandel (1980) have outlined a molecular model for sensitization: Serotonin released by facilitating neurons acting on a serotonin receptor sets up a biochemical cascade within presynaptic terminals of the sensory cell. The receptor activates a serotonin-sensitive adenylate cyclase, which increases cyclic AMP in the terminals. The cyclic AMP in turn activates a protein kinase—an enzyme that phosphorylates proteins, the latter reaction in turn changes the three-dimensional shape of the protein and therefore its functional state. The phosphorylations in this reaction affect a specific species of potassium channel protein-reducing potassium currents that normally repolarize the action potential. This closing of the potassium channel results in prolonged action potential, which in turn results in the calcium channel remaining open longer, thus allowing more Ca^{++} to flow into the terminal. More vesicles bind to release sites and more transmitter is released, increasing the functional output of the cell. The animal then shows more responsiveness.

CHAPTER 10

Where in the Brain
Are Memories Stored?

WHERE IN THE BRAIN are memories stored? Admittedly, the task of shifting from the complex abstract conceptual framework of symbolic meanings and nodal memory networks to the discrete cell biology of "Pavlovian indoctrination" in *Aplysia* and the startle reflex in the rat has been difficult. Moving next to studies of the neural substrata of more complex memory systems may be even more difficult, but at the same time more evocative of clinical psychoanalytic interest. The topic of affects enters here to complicate and enliven the task. The manifestations of affect in both realms (mind and brain-body) are so immediate as to render particularly urgent a felt need to accomplish the impossible task of discussing and understanding them in both languages at once, but despite this we'll have to approach from one side at a time.

To summarize from the psychoanalytic side, shared affect or affective potential is conceived to function as the "glue" or "binding" that organizes associative memory networks such as that uncovered in Carol by the progressive work of the psychoanalytic process. From the psychoanalytic side, avoidance of unpleasant (psychically painful) affects is regarded as reason for instigating psychological defense mechanisms in response to an attenuated physiologic discharge (signal anxiety). The latter announces a danger situation, which has the potential to generate intensely painful affect ("traumatic situation") if mental representation of the conflicted idea(s) is not barred by defensive mental operations from explicit conscious recognition and access to expression by the motor apparatus.

On the neurobiologic side, the field of cognitive neuropsychology, especially the neurobiology of cognitive development in nonhuman primates, provides exciting and important data. For our purposes, I propose to focus mainly on selected findings from two leading programs of investigation in nonhuman primates—one mainly on adult animals, headed by Mortimer Mishkin, and the other mainly on developing infant and young animals, headed by Patricia Goldman-Rakic. Interestingly, both developed from earlier work in the same laboratory (the Laboratory of Neuropsychology at the National Institute of Mental Health when that laboratory was headed by H. E. Rosvold). These programs have taken full advantage of new technologies whereby it is possible to combine sophisticated and complex but precisely manipulable behavioral methods (for example, cognitive tasks such as the delayed response task) with newly developed neurobiologic methods. These latter include anatomic methods for study of structures, regions, and connections; physiologic methods for study of single cell and cell population activity in specified areas of brain; neurochemical methods for study of neurotransmitter (e.g., monoamine) systems, including effects of neuropharmacologic agents; and metabolic methods (e.g., 2-deoxyglucose metabolic labeling for study of metabolic activity in specified brain regions). These new technologies make it possible to delineate more specifically than ever before neural substrata of specific cognitive functions and to assess separate and interactive effects of lesions, drugs, toxins, development, aging, and *experience.* Both programs of investigation clearly indicate that in addition to primary cortical projection areas, multisynaptic cortico-cortical (association) pathways are involved in processing sensory visual input.

Two Systems of Memory?

Mishkin's brilliant work, carried out over many years and with many colleagues, has identified two such cortico-cortical pathways, each involving several hierarchically arranged cortical areas. One pathway goes from the occipital visual cortex dorsally to the frontal motor system; the other, of more interest in this context, goes ventrally to the temporal limbic system. The fibers in the ventral pathways are modality specific and are important for stimulus recognition and meaning (Spiegler and Mishkin 1981). Mishkin states that recognition of a stimulus depends not only on passage along this ventral cortical pathway but also on storage of a central representation of the stimulus in that pathway's last station in the anterior tempero-insular region, which projects directly to the amygdala and indirectly to the hippocampus. These latter two (limbic) structures project to the medial thalamus. Mishkin concludes that storage of the central representation of a stimulus occurs only if this cortico-limbic-thalamic pathway is activated and that once the central representation of a stimulus has been stored it can enter into association with the stored representations of other stimuli and other events. According to these findings, then, it appears that it is through the cortico-amygdal-thalamic interactions that stimulus-affect associations occur, thereby providing the stimulus with meaning.

This sort of memory function is of high interest to clinicians, especially psychoanalytic clinicians. Readers wishing to pursue these ideas in further detail will find it worthwhile to consult Mishkin's (1982) published formulation, "A Memory System in the Monkey." In it, a neural model is presented, based largely on evidence from studies in monkeys, postulating that coded representations of stimuli are stored in the higher-order sensory (i.e., association) areas of the cortex whenever stimulus activation of these areas also triggers a cortico-limbo-thalamo-cortical circuit. This circuit, which could act as either an imprinting or rehearsal mechanism, may actually consist of two parallel circuits, one involving the amygdala and the dorsomedial nucleus of the thalamus, and the other the hippocampus and the anterior nuclei. The stimulus representation stored in cortex by action of these circuits is seen as mediating three different memory processes: recognition, which occurs when the stored representation is reactivated via the original sensory pathway; recall, when it is reactivated via any other pathway; and association, when it activates other stored representations (sensory, affective, spatial, motor) via the outputs of the higher-order sensory areas to the relevant structures (Mishkin 1982, p. 85).

More recently his group has uncovered evidence that leads them to postulate a second system, in which stimulus representations stored in the cortex are connected to the striatal complex or basal ganglia. This cortico-striatal system appears to function independently of and in parallel with the cortico-limbic memory system just described. Mishkin calls this cortico-striatal system a *habit* system, since it involves *noncognitive links* to subcortical structures. He tentatively proposes that since the striatal complex is older than the limbic system and cortex (i.e., precedes them in phylogenesis), it would be reasonable to assume that it precedes them in ontogenesis as well. This proposal is indeed supported by developmental studies of infant monkeys. Speculating further, Mishkin (1982) asks if the learning process is actually shared by the two systems—the one for what he terms "habit memory" (referring to learned motor responses that occur without stimulus recognition) and the other for cognitive memory as we know it. How might they both cooperate and conflict with each other?

Following in his speculative vein, I can't resist offering a first tentative probe for correspondence between the mental and physiologic realms: Could there be a fundamental analogy between this postulated principle of dual—parallel and independent—physiologic systems that process two types of learning and Freud's idea of two parallel and independent modes (primary and secondary) of processing information in the mental realm—in both instances one mode older than the other and closer to primitive than to complex cognitive functions? None of this should sound strange or foreign to psychoanalytic students of memory, especially as manifest in dreams.

Role of the Prefrontal Cortex

But there is more: an extensive series of highly innovative, imaginative, and technically dazzling studies by Patricia Goldman-Rakic and her colleagues. Among other accomplishments, these studies have added immeasurably to an appreciation of the anatomic, physiologic, and behavioral plasticity displayed by the developing nervous system, and to knowledge concerning developmental neurochemistry and the role of the dopaminergic system in the function of the prefrontal association cortex, which plays such a central role in cognition.

The main behavioral paradigm used in this program of studies to assess prefrontal cognitive function was the *Delayed Response Task,* which is *the* classical marker for functional integrity of the prefrontal association cortex. In it the subject is allowed to observe an experimenter bait one of two recessed wells with food. Both wells are then covered and a screen interposed between the wells and the subject. When the screen is raised, the subject is allowed to open one well, and if it has remembered the correct choice, to retrieve the food reward, or otherwise, to go unrewarded. In a variation of the test, *Delayed Alternation* (also used in these studies), the subject is required to alternate between left and right food wells on successive trials which are separated by delay periods. In the latter task, the subject's choice on any given trial is predicated on *faithful memory* of the preceding choice.

The Delayed Alternation test of spatial delayed reaction has been proven useful in study of brain damage, pharmacologic treatment, aging, and development. This task provided the first behavioral demonstration of deficits in memory function attributable to a localized region of the central nervous system. Spatial delay memory tasks are relatively quickly mastered by normal adult monkeys; adult lobectomized monkeys perform only at chance levels:

> The dependence of the delayed response upon prefrontal cortex is considered one of the best and most solidly established structure-function relationships in neuropsychology. The elemental capacity to recognize that an object exists despite its temporary disappearance reflects an ability to behave in terms of anticipated or remembered outcome. Such an ability has to be considered a building block, if not the very cornerstone of cognitive development. The delayed response task certainly resembles the object permanence task which has been used so extensively in children [Piaget 1954] (Goldman-Rakic et al. 1983).

In regard to maturation in the monkey, it has been shown that the delayed response capabilities mature at a relatively late point in ontogeny, suggesting that the prefrontal cortex does not assume its mature role in this respect until relatively late in *postnatal* life. In the review just cited, it is suggested that "the demonstration that a portion of the cerebral cortex concerned with selective cognitive processes does not become functionally mature until or after puberty may be relevant to neurological mechanisms involved in human cognition which likewise do not become fully functionally mature until or after puberty." Again this seems consonant with Piaget's findings.

More About How Memories May Be Stored in the Brain

It is particularly interesting that dopamine, which is known to play an important role in expression of emotional and cognitive behaviors in the human, has been shown, in studies by members of the same research group, to be particularly important in the functions subserved by the prefrontal cortex (Brozoski et al. 1979). In young adult rhesus monkeys, catecholamine levels vary across cortical regions. Dopamine concentration is highest in the prefrontal cortex and then is found in progressively lower concentrations along the anterior-posterior axis of the brain, reaching the lowest level in visual cortex at the occipital pole. The patterns of cortical distribution of norepinephrine and serotonin concentrations are quite different. Brozoski et al. (1979) were intrigued by the idea that high concentrations of dopamine in prefrontal association cortex of the rhesus monkey might mean that dopamine plays some role in processing spatial memory capacities of this part of the brain. To test this idea, they selectively depleted the prefrontal cortex of monkeys of dopamine and then tested their spatial memory capacities.

Before drug treatments, the monkeys were trained both on a delayed alternation task (to ascertain how long they could retain spatial information in memory) and on a visual discrimination task, which did not involve spatial memory. Following baseline determinations, subjects were pretreated with DMI, a substance that protects norepinephrine terminals, and then injections of 6-hydroxy dopamine were made directly into the prefrontal cortex. 6-hydroxy dopamine selectively destroys the axon terminals of catecholamine neurons. When 6-hydroxy dopamine is given after pretreatment with DMI, a selective reduction of dopamine content results.

The experimental animals after recovery displayed normal motor and appetitive behavior. But on retesting, the dopamine-depleted animals showed a profound deficit in delayed alternation performance—approaching in severity that shown by animals with surgical lesions of prefrontal cortex. At the same time, these subjects continued to perform the visual discrimination task (not involving spatial memory) at pretreatment levels. Administration of L-Dopa returned their alternation performance to predeficit levels. Depletion of either norepinephrine or serotonin in control animals produced slight if any effect on alternation performance. Together, these findings implicate an important role for dopamine in the prefrontal cognitive (memory) function. Once again, we encounter a mono-amine neurotransmitter when we zero in on "memory" from the neurobiologic side!

This condensed resume of Goldman-Rakic's work, being selective and focused, conveys the words but not the "music." To correct this, let me refer to a somewhat more speculative paper (Goldman and Rakic 1979). Here, the authors state, "It is important to emphasize that evidence for modification of higher centers in the developing primate brain is not limited to studies which impose traumatic injury" (p. 25). They cite (1) both recovery from early brain injury and the developmental effects of selective early training on neural cognitive development and (2) the role of gonadal hormones in development of cognitive and social competence as examples of neural plasticity and as providing

evidence that the structure and pattern of neuronal connections are genetically determined but can be altered by various influences from the outside world including unbalanced sensory experience—in other words, immature connections require functional validation. ... It is not known whether such a process occurs by establishment of new synaptic contacts or as a result of changes in the biochemistry and functional parameters of existing synapses. It is clear that detecting the mechanisms by which experience influences the development of neural connections, synaptogenesis, and function is a major challenge for modern neurobiology (Goldman and Rakic 1979, pp. 25–26).

Note the similarity of these ideas to Kandel's concept (chapter 9) that genetic programming predetermines the establishment and patterning of synaptic connections while developmental experience influences their functional strength and stability. It seems quite reasonable to regard the phenotype as expressing the functional synthesized product of interaction between the genotype and experience, especially experiences occurring during critical phases (critical periods) of development.

To summarize, some "first approximation" answers to the questions *where* in the brain and *how* may memories be stored have been reviewed in this chapter and the preceding one.

Neurobiologic, neuroanatomic, neuropsychologic, and neuro-pharmacologic studies in adult and developing monkeys have demonstrated that sensory percepts registered in primary cortical projection areas are first processed along a complex series of cortical association pathways. If they are then connected with affect systems through bidirectional cortico-limbic pathways, they can be retained for recall in association with percepts stored in cortex and in this way acquire meaning. Elemental memory processes are dependent on prefrontal association cortex, and these memory functions depend on the presence of the neurotransmitter dopamine. These primate studies tell us something about *where* in brain memory processes occur and also a bit about how. Combined behavioral, neurophysiologic, neuropharmacologic, cell biologic, and molecular genetic studies in the marine snail *Aplysia* tell us about *how* learning and experience may lead to changes in function and eventually to changes in specified aspects of structure of individual presynaptic sensory neurons.

Regulation of the intracellular cascade of neurochemical changes within the individual neuron is effected by intracellular enzymatic actions. The enzymes involved are also programmed originally by genes. Some of these enzymatic functions may also be subject to modification by learning and experience. It is this latter possibility that has led Kandel and Schwartz (1982) to speculate about the existence of "a basic molecular grammar of memory."

A Probe

This is a good juncture at which to speculate a bit and see if it is worthwhile to let ideas from the two sides—psychoanalysis and neurobiology—speak to each other, remembering that the languages, methods, and units are different on the two sides. The idea is not to find identity but to see if it seems feasible to induce reciprocal enrichment and complementary enhancement of progress separately on each side. It may be too soon to judge—I shall leave it to you to decide.

Remember Carol's subway phobia? We psychoanalyzed it with quite a satisfactory outcome; in doing so, we encountered a repressed, affectively charged, conflictful core memory that was embedded, so to speak, in the "structure" of the phobia. Remembering it coincided with recovery. We now know (long after Carol's phobia) that patients with certain types of panic disorders and associated circumscribed phobias may respond very favorably to administration of tricyclic antidepressant drugs and, sometimes even more favorably, to monoamine oxidase inhibitors (MAOIs). Both classes of drugs increase available monoamines in the brain, including SEROTONIN and DOPAMINE. If MAOIs and tricyclic antidepressants had been available at the time of Carol's panic and instantaneous subway phobia, would they have helped? I do not mean to suggest that drugs and psychotherapy are mutually interchangeable forms of treatment, nor am I suggesting that drug-induced symptomatic effects would provide a preferable alternative to psychotherapy. My intent is to call attention to the fact that a correct psychoanalytic interpretation effected cure of a condition that might also have responded symptomatically to a very different treatment modality, namely, administration of a pharmacologic agent with a known neuropharmacologic mode of action, but the relation of the pharmacologic mechanism to the symptom change is not entirely clear. And I am asking whether, and if so to what extent, similar or common basic mechanisms could be involved when similar results can be brought about by these very different treatment modalities. One cannot help but wonder about the neurochemical dynamics and kinetics of neurotransmitter systems in areas of the brain known to be associated with memory functions—and their possible relationships to the psychodynamics of motivated forgetting and remembering.

Referring back to the explicit rationale that was stated earlier (chapter 2) for undertaking dual-track probes such as this one, I would regard the two data sets in this specific example as supplementing and complementing each other in a worthwhile way. When considered together, they do suggest mutualities and resemblances and they do point in directions worthy of future study. We are just beginning to sense the complexities of centrally active neurotransmitter substances (how many are there and of what chemical types?) and the complexities of neurotransmitter systems and of their various interrelationships: with one another and with membrane receptors, with the cell biology of pre- and postsynaptic neurons, and so forth. I do not mean to focus on a few specific substances such as particular biogenic amines and on a few particular structures and anatomical systems and so imply that enlightenment is close at hand. But I cannot help casting a wistful and wishful glance at psychoanalytically exposed nodal memory networks when I think about interrelated neurotransmitter systems, neuronal networks, and systems of functionally organized brain structures. In this respect the empirical data on the neuroscience side is way ahead. Will we succeed in finding better (more compatible) ways to organize data on the psychoanalytic side so that it can discourse more effectively with the biological?

CHAPTER 11

The Psychoanalytic Theory of Signal Anxiety and the Pavlovian Paradigm of the Conditioned Response: Toward an Empirical Articulation

IN the John Flynn Memorial Lecture, "From Metapsychology to Molecular Biology: Explorations into the Nature of Anxiety," Kandel (1983) noted that evidence adducing to the fact that anxiety is inborn and that a neutral stimulus can be associated with it through learning originates in comparative and evolutionary biology (Darwin 1873; Romanes 1883, 1888). These ideas were followed by William James' (1893) proposal that built-in inherited defensive behaviors are triggered by anxiety, and finally, by Pavlov's (1927) assertion that defensive reflexes can be modified by experience. In the Flynn lecture, Kandel also noted the similarity of Freud's theory of signal anxiety to the foregoing ideas, and commented on the fact that both Pavlov and Freud realized that not only could anxiety be learned but "the ability to manifest anticipatory defensive responses to danger signals is biologically adaptive" (p. 1278).

Physiological stress response mechanisms, originally developed for dealing with external danger and tuned to external input channels, have in man evolved to a point where they are also activated internally, and so are tuned to internal input channels as well. The evolutionary survival advantage of the capacity to anticipate danger and generate proactive responses may well have been the factor that supported the development of cognitive functions and their link-up with the (original) physiologic stress response system. Emotions, as the product of this link-up, are inseparably part of both the realm of meaning and the realm of physiochemical biology.

Brain-body in humans can be regarded as a single apparatus subserving responses to challenges emanating from two disparate (physical and nonphysical) components of the environment. Thus, we are challenged: how to understand one response system that is capable of generating integrated responses to two disparate input systems and to each in its "own terms." How may such a system have developed? As we have seen in chapter 9, simple animal models of anxiety can be and have been studied in amazingly precise behavioral, neuropsychologic, neuropharmacologic, and cell biologic detail. In chapter 8 I proposed that it would be worthwhile to rethink aspects of psychoanalytic theory so as to recast them into forms still consonant with their empirical bases in psychoanalytic work but also consonant with concepts and phenomena under study in the biological sciences. Such efforts, if successful, should facilitate conceptual and empirical articulation between the disciplines.

It should come as no surprise, then, that Kandel's (1983)

Flynn lecture and his experimental studies of models of anxiety in *Aplysia* inspired me to attempt a detailed recasting of Freud's centrally important theory of signal anxiety into the Pavlovian paradigm, with the heuristic aim of bringing it into meaningful—perhaps even empirical—articulation with current neurobiologic data and thinking. This chapter, then, asks whether conceptual recasting of that aspect of the theory might in fact accomplish the goal of suggesting or promoting mutually worthwhile directions for empirical research.

Recasting the Theory

To recapitulate Freud's theory (1926) of signal anxiety, it postulates two concomitant parallel lines of development and maturation (see figure 11.1): one in the psychological realm involving cognitive function, the other in the physiologic realm involving the autonomic and neuroendocrine apparatus. On the cognitive psychological side, Freud postulated a developing cognitive capacity to respond to inner and/or outer stimuli as constituting danger situations, that is, situations with the potential to develop into "traumatic situations." Inner stimuli were conceived as consisting of drive-derived motives which, if recognized and carried out, would generate a situation in which the organism would be overwhelmed and rendered helpless, a situation analogous to the original "traumatic situation" of birth.

As the infant/child matured, the psychic meaning and content of the danger changed from mother's absence, to loss of mother's love, to fear of genital injury (castration), to fear of severe punishment by inner conscience (superego). Freud postulated further the laying down during mental development of networks of memory traces—residual, enduring engrams of actually experienced or fantasized events connected in time with conflicted situations and hence with the potential to generate the same kinds of affective responses. The signaling "system," then, could be activated from inside by inner needs or

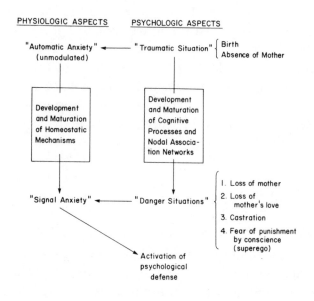

PHYSIOLOGIC ASPECTS   PSYCHOLOGIC ASPECTS

"Automatic Anxiety" ◄——— "Traumatic Situation" { Birth
(unmodulated)   Absence of Mother

Development   Development
and Maturation   and Maturation
of Homeostatic   of Cognitive
Mechanisms   Processes and
                     Nodal Associa-
                     tion Networks

"Signal Anxiety" ◄——— "Danger Situations"   { 1. Loss of mother
                                              2. Loss of
                                                 mother's love
                                              3. Castration
                                              4. Fear of punishment
                                                 by conscience
                                                 (superego)

                         Activation of
                         psychological
                         defense

FIGURE 11.1.
The Ontogeny of Signal Anxiety

from outside by meaningful life situations—situations that
have sufficient analogous or homologous meaningful resemblance to those important earlier unresolved conflictual situations which had left traces in the nodal memory network.

On the physiologic side, Freud postulated progressive developmental maturation of homeostatic mechanisms (such as
baroreceptor feedback mechanisms) which, when fully developed and functional, would "tame" the uncontrolled, chaotic
physiologic responses of early infancy and convert them to
modulated, finely tuned, autonomically innervated reactions.
Perception of these small physiologic perturbations (sometimes even subliminally) would signal danger and call psychological defense mechanisms into operation in order to avert
escalation to a "traumatic situation" and "automatic anxiety."
This development of signal anxiety is schematically illustrated
in figures 11.3–11.10.

Figure 11.2 depicts the familiar Pavlovian paradigm as originally studied in the dog. Both the previously neutral conditioned stimulus (CS-tone) and the unconditioned stimulus (US-shock) are external. Before conditioning, the tone produces no response and the electric shock to the paw produces an internal physiologic bodily response. This is the unconditioned response (UR), exemplified in the figure by increase in heart rate. The dog also reacts behaviorally, withdrawing its paw—or attacking the apparatus. After conditioning, accomplished by precisely specified temporal pairing of external stimuli (tone with shock), the CS alone produces the conditioned physiologic response—increase in heart rate—(CR) *and* withdrawal of the paw.

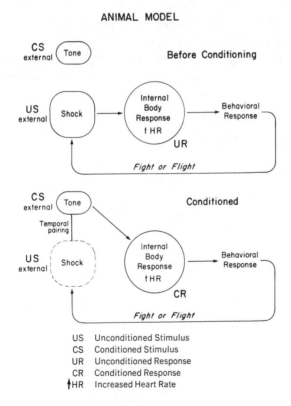

ANIMAL MODEL

US	Unconditioned Stimulus
CS	Conditioned Stimulus
UR	Unconditioned Response
CR	Conditioned Response
↑HR	Increased Heart Rate

FIGURE 11.2
The Pavlovian Paradigm

In the human infant, a number of additional steps must be visualized in conceptualizing the development of the signal anxiety mechanism. The top half of figure 11.3 depicts the inborn reaction to the original "traumatic situation" (birth—separation from the mother) as an intense internal physiologic body response, "automatic anxiety," accompanied by behavioral helplessness. The bottom half of the figure allows a comparison to the animal's inborn response to an external trauma (shock).

Figure 11.4 depicts the first two postulated steps in the evolution of signal anxiety. The top diagram depicts the analogue of the unconditioned state in the animal model. The conditioned stimulus (CS_1) consists of the instinctual need (I) not yet paired with the conditioned stimulus (US_1)—the "traumatic situation," the analogue of the electric shock which is not yet paired with the CS-tone. Note that here both CS_1 and US_1 are internal rather than external as in the animal model.

The lower diagram depicts the infantile analogue of conditioning in the animal. In the infant's experience the traumatic

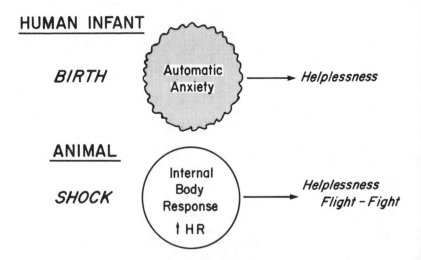

FIGURE 11.3
The "Traumatic Situation"

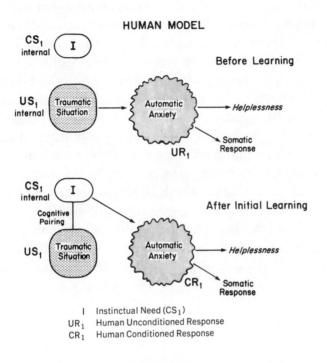

FIGURE 11.4
Pavlovian Paradigm: Human Model—Initial Learning

situation can be thought of as the unconditioned stimulus (US_1) which generates automatic anxiety—analogous to shock (US) which generates an internal physiologic response in the animal. The emerging instinctual derivative or need (I) is the analogue of the conditioned stimulus in the animal. In other words, CS_1 is analogous to CS; it now can alone produce the conditioned response (CR_1, automatic anxiety).

Schematizing the development in this way illuminates two points of difference from the animal model:

1. Both CS_1 and US_1 are internal rather than external as in the animal.
2. Conditioning takes places by virtue of an internal (cognitive) process—an experiential cognitive pairing of internal events, rather than experimentally manipulated temporal pairing of the external events as in the animal.

Otherwise, the situation can be seen as quite parallel to that of the animal model. Figure 11.5 depicts this comparison.

The next development, depicted in figure 11.6, entails adding a more advanced cognitive step—cognitive anticipatory pairing. This postulates development of the ability to conceive of a "danger situation" as a situation having the potential to develop into a "traumatic situation." This cognitive ability would modify the psychological impact of the conditioned stimulus (emerging instinctual need—I) at the same time that the internal physiologic response was starting to undergo a parallel process of attenuation, which is depicted schematically as half-accomplished—half "automatic" (labeled CR_1) and half "signal" (labeled CR_2). The unconditioned stimulus is also depicted schematically in figure 11.6 as half and half—half "danger situation" (US_2) and half "traumatic situation" (US_1). At

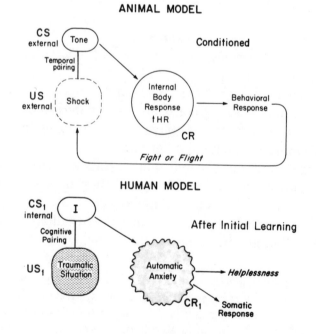

FIGURE 11.5
Initial Learning: Human and Animal Models Compared

this stage the physiologic response serves to initiate or stimulate mental activity. The infant is no longer totally helpless. The physiologic response serves as a motivational state giving rise to primitive defenses—internal psychological mechanisms which can be regarded as mental equivalents of fight-flight behavior in the animal. The latter was directed against the external source of pain in the animal; in the developing human the psychological defenses are directed against the internal source of psychic pain.

The next step is visualized in figure 11.7, which portrays the penultimate form of the human analogue of the conditioned response in the animal model. Its comparison with the animal model appears in figure 11.8.

1. The conditioned stimulus is still depicted as the same—a pressing instinctual need.

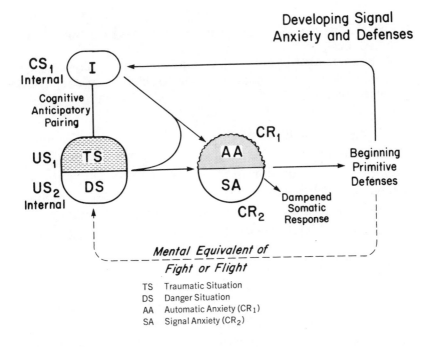

FIGURE 11.6

Human Model: Developing Signal Anxiety and Defenses

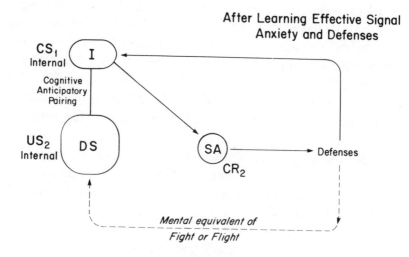

FIGURE 11.7
Penultimate Human Model

2. US_2, the "danger situation," now predominates at the internal cognitive level.
3. Fully attenuated signal anxiety (CR_2) now is the physiologic response to the conditioned stimulus (I), mobilizing effective defenses against it.

One further cognitive developmental step must be visualized as taking place (probably in parallel with the foregoing steps) before the final situation in the human can be schematized. It is the link-up between the nodal associative network of stored memories that share affective potential with each other and the emerging conflicted need-I (CS_1). This can be thought of as generalization in Pavlovian terminology. As depicted in figure 11.9 and figure 11.10, which compares the final human model with the animal model, this nodal associative memory system would be capable of activation both from within, by an emerging conflicted instinctual motive (I), and from without, by a meaningful external (psychosocial) situation. And when activated, it is postulated (alone or in concert with conflicted instinctual motives) to initiate the signal anxiety mechanism

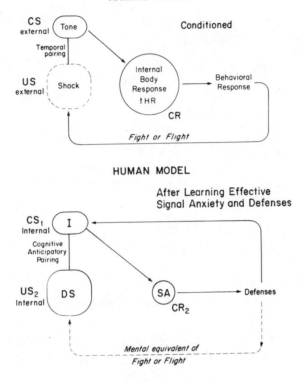

FIGURE 11.8

Animal Model and Penultimate Human Model Compared

which, in turn, mobilizes psychological defenses against internal and/or external (social, environmental, intrapersonal) sources of danger. Those directed solely at internal stimulation would be manifest primarily in intrapsychic phenomena; those directed at external situations would in addition manifest themselves in adaptively motivated coping behavior intended to ameliorate the external problem(s).

Breakdown of defensive functions (figure 11.11) could be regarded as analogous to the developmental stage depicted in figure 11.6 with (1) generation of enough "free" clinical anxiety (CR_1—physiologic mobilization) to contribute to behavioral and physiologic "stress" responses and disorders, and (2) acti-

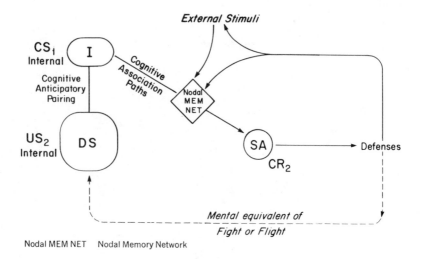

Nodal MEM NET   Nodal Memory Network

FIGURE 11.9
Final Human Model

vation of regressive, more primitive psychopathological defenses such as those encountered in patients with clinical psychiatric disorders.

Total breakdown of defenses (figure 11.12) would lead to a situation comparable to that depicted in the lower half of figure 11.4, with psychotic panic and helplessness—plus uncontrolled physiologic activation (automatic anxiety) CR_1.

In summary, signal anxiety can be regarded in a Pavlovian paradigm as the (attenuated) analogue of the original unconditioned response (automatic anxiety)—attenuated by virtue of (1) the psychic (cognitive) replacement of the original stimulus, the "traumatic situation," by the "danger situation," and (2) the parallel development of psychological defenses as mental equivalents of fight or flight. Such a scheme makes it reasonable to think of signal anxiety as an evolutionary modification of the composite physiologic-behavioral response to external danger displayed by animals throughout the phylogenetic scale. Realizing that such a recasting of the concept of signal anxiety does not add new explanatory depth, I nevertheless suggest that it should make the concept easier to think about

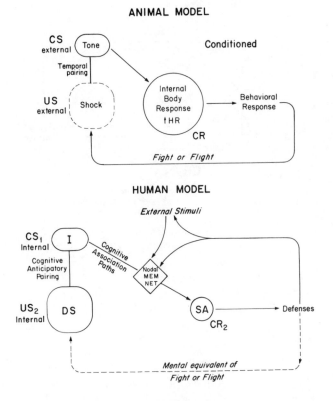

ANIMAL MODEL

HUMAN MODEL

FIGURE 11.10
Animal and Fully Mature (Final) Human Models Compared

in a broader biological context and to study both in the clinic and in the laboratory.

More Questions from Parent Discipline to Antidiscipline

When and how does the "instinct" impinge on the mental realm as a drive-motivated impulse and link up (if it in fact does) as a conditioned stimulus with the mental version of the uncondi-

137

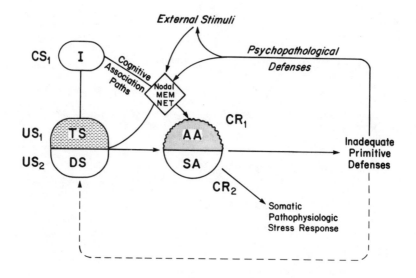

FIGURE 11.11
Human Model: Partial Breakdown of Defenses

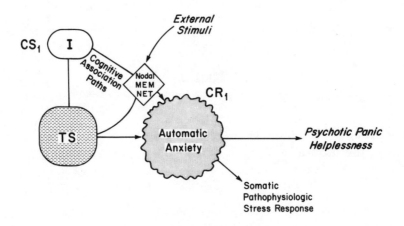

FIGURE 11.12
Human Model: Total Breakdown of Defenses

tioned stimulus, that is, "the traumatic situation"? What is the developmental timetable of autonomic maturation? When do various homeostatic mechanisms mature and begin to function? Would such times constitute "critical periods" with significance for later pathogenic reactions?

To answer some of these questions, it might be useful and should now be possible to add systematic concomitant physiologic measurements to already sophisticated cognitive and behavioral techniques in studies of developing human (and nonhuman primate) neonates and young infants. Such measurements could even permit some planned experimental manipulation. The human infant would be worthwhile to study as it displays early "startle" and global anxiety responses, and later "stranger anxiety," "practice," and "rapprochement" behaviors during the separation-individuation phase (Mahler et al. 1975). Would it be possible systematically to observe and quantify sequential cognitive and physiologic developmental changes such as those postulated in Freud's theory of signal anxiety? In the nonhuman primates, additional advantages could be offered by opportunities for neuropharmacologic analyses of neural substrate mechanisms.

Even in simple organisms, it might well be appropriate and worthwhile to study additional behaviors and somatic functions displayed by *Aplysia* experiencing this "learned motivational state" (Kandel 1978). This would help to develop a fuller inventory of organismic responses in this highly important model system, which may well constitute the basic model and module on which and from which more complex functions in higher forms may have evolved. Additional detail at this level might suggest leads as to what to look for in studies of more complex behaviors and responses in more complex organisms.

CHAPTER 12

Evaluating and Reacting to Danger: The Psychophysiology of Stress

IN MOVING toward consideration of the clinical (medical and psychiatric) implications of the issues we have been discussing, we can use the stress response as a logical stepping-off point. But a word of caution is in order. The chapter subtitle, "Psychophysiology of Stress," is in the strictest sense a mistitle. The subject will be discussed almost entirely in the language and data of physiology, even though it is well established that the stress response can be elicited both in animals and humans by psychological as well as by physical, chemical, infectious, neoplastic, and other such stressors. This assertion rests on a vast literature, beginning with the work of Cannon (1915) and then of Selye (1946) and most recently reviewed comprehensively in an important new volume edited by Goldberger and Breznitz (1982). The clinical relevance and importance of psychosocial factors in maintaining states of health and contributing to pathogenesis of disease in humans is clear. That is not what is at issue. What *is* at issue is the still missing "gap" in knowledge referred that would, if available, enable us to relate data from the two realms (mind and brain-body) to each other.

In animal work, quantitative dimensions of psychological and psychosocial stress can often be manipulated with precision, but qualitative dimensions must most often be handled either in a global generic sense or by "operational" inferences based on behavioral observations. Though these inferences may be quite reasonable—even highly sophisticated—they cannot reflect what is actually in the animal's mind. We have not yet learned to communicate with animals about such matters. And in virtually all experimental studies in the human, there is also an understandable but nonetheless empirically serious incongruity between psychological and physiologic data. Judging by idealistic and perfectionist standards, we simply do not have available for study satisfactorily full and deep psychodynamic descriptions of the mental activities accompanying physiologic states that can be and have been studied in precise detail by highly sophisticated, modern neurobiologic techniques. Consequently, we do not have a step-by-step explication of exactly how nonphysical stimuli (meanings) are transduced into pathogenic physical events in brain-body. There seem to be plenty of connections and mechanisms that we already know about for accomplishing this. We know how it could happen, but until (if ever) we know exactly how it does happen, we will not have the full explanations that would enable us clinically to choose and deploy psychological and physical therapeutic interventions separately or in specified combinations with full understanding, precision, and accuracy. To be able to do so would raise clinical practice to a near-ideal level and surely we should be striving to attain it.

The preceding chapters of this book have endeavored to convey (1) the richness and complexity of the human's inner mental life and the sense of the order these mental processes can display when studied by the psychoanalytic method, and

(2) the modular compatibility of that sense of order (specifically in respect to memory function and anxiety) with models derived from a wide range of neurobiologic strategies and methods extending from cell biology of "learning" at one end to developmental neurobiology of cognition at the other.

The chapters to follow are not intended to provide a comprehensive review of what used to be called "psychosomatic medicine." (For such a review, see H. Weiner, *Psychobiology and Human Disease,* 1977.) Rather, they will, as have previous chapters, focus discussion on some selected areas of research in neurobiology. Specifically, they will examine ways in which study of central nervous system mechanisms may expand our understanding of biological processes that lead to disease. I will not attempt to bring them into close or immediate articulation with the much broader field of detailed information, reviewed by Weiner, about the general biology of disease and the etiology and pathogenesis of specific diseases affecting organ systems and tissues outside the brain. That would be a task beyond the scope of this volume and, it goes without saying, of its author. But I will in these chapters attempt to lead in the direction of constructing a heuristic model that might serve as a framework for relating previous research and theory about mind-brain and brain-body relationships in health and disease to a constantly and rapidly expanding data base and to more recent conceptual models—even, perhaps, to anticipate what may be promising new directions.

From the Psychoanalytic Side

Before going on to the psychophysiology of stress and its broader clinical implications for psychosomatic and clinical psychiatric theory, let me lead you up to each side of the brink. As already noted, however, affects involved in the stress response are manifest so immediately in both mental and biological realms that it is difficult to discuss them entirely in "pure" form from either of the two sides alone. Admittedly, this fact constitutes a serious challenge for the "dual-track approach."

From the psychoanalytic side, let's review briefly chapter 11, which presented a detailed recasting of the psychoanalytic theory of signal anxiety (including its ontogenetic developmental aspects) into a form congruent with the Pavlovian paradigm. You will recall that the theory, which is empirically based primarily on psychological observations, nonetheless extrapolates to the physiologic realm. Signal anxiety is postulated to be an attenuated (physiologically mild but detectable) version of the vigorous, overwhelming infantile physiologic response (automatic anxiety) to a traumatic situation (one in which the infant was passively overwhelmed with stimuli that it could not control or handle). In the course of development and maturation, this automatic anxiety response is considered to undergo progressive taming. (From the physiologic side, we know that developmental maturation of neurovegetative homeostatic mechanisms, e.g., baroreceptor reflexes, is part of postnatal developmental epochs, although the details of the timetable are yet to be filled in as far as I know.)

Psychoanalytic theory postulates parallel developmental maturation of cognitive mechanisms to enable recognition of psychological danger situations and anticipation of their potential to lead to a state like the original traumatic situation. Additionally, and in parallel with cognitive and physiologic maturational changes, psychological defense mechanisms are thought to develop and to be activated in response to the anxiety signal. Their role is to prevent conflicted ideas (contained in networks of memory traces linked by shared capacity to generate psychically painful affects) from attaining recognition in consciousness and access to motor systems for expression in behavior.

When psychological defenses fail partially (reflected in psychopathological manifestations), the attenuated physiologic response is conceived to become more active again; total breakdown of defenses would eventuate in a repetition of a state analogous to the infantile one. "Reactivation" of the immature and more vigorous physiologic responses can and has been postulated by many investigators to be involved in the somatic pathophysiologic sequelae of the "stress response." In this connection we need only cite the empirically well-established reciprocal relationship between effectiveness of psychological defenses and vigor of neuroendocrine responses measured under stressful conditions. This phenomenon, first demonstrated by Sachar and colleagues (1963) in studies on patients with acute schizophrenic excitement, has been repeatedly replicated in a wide variety of studies of patients under acute and chronic stressful situations. In all of these studies, psychological assessment of defenses and laboratory measurement of neuroendocrine function were carried out independently of each other, and only afterward correlated. These are covariance data and do not, of course, indicate causal sequences; the idea of causal sequences may well be irrelevant and unnecessary, and is contrary to thinking in systems terms.

Based on clinical data from the psychoanalytic side, psychologically induced stress can be conceptualized as a condition in which psychological defense mechanisms must be mobilized in response to inner stimuli (conflicted drive-derived motives) and/or outer (interpersonal psychological and psychosocial) stimuli or events which activate dormant elements in conflictual memory networks. The balance between the threatening and defensive "forces" can be upset by any or all of the following:

1. Sudden upsurge of drive motives as in adolescence and menopause
2. Weakening of defenses as may occur in altered states of consciousness or in toxic, physically debilitating states, or as may occur in response to interpretive work in analysis (remember Carol's "secret" abdominal symptom and her response to my interpretation of the underlying wish that it expressed)
3. A life situation that bears such marked resemblance to an intense past conflictual situation as to revive its memory traces and associated conflicted motives (remember Carol's responses to starting analysis, to her brother's burn in the tapioca incident, to the move of the analyst's office, and to the impending death of her grandmother).

Such are the complexities of the human condition to which the full dimension of responses to the terms "psychological and psychosocial stress" refer. These complexities provide the context in which these terms should be understood.

But as noted earlier, psychoanalytic theory extrapolates to postulated phenomena in the physiologic realm, that is, to "traumatic anxiety" and "signal anxiety." We've now come to the brink—or edge of the gap—approaching from the psychoanalytic side.

To investigate and clarify the relationship (or lack of it) between the postulated and the actual biology of anxiety constitutes a challenge not only for psychoanalysis but also for basic neurobiology and, because of its implications for the stress responses, for general clinical medicine and psychiatry.

What does it look like on the neurobiologic side?

From the Neurobiologic Side

The evolutionary adaptive value of a mechanism for signaling approaching or potential danger or for evoking measures to avoid and/or to counteract it was recognized by Pavlov and Freud as well as by earlier workers in psychology and in comparative and evolutionary biology (see chapter 11).

A prior requirement for development and function of such a mechanism would be the capacity to receive, evaluate, code, and store for retrieval informational input both from inside and outside the organism. Recent studies, specified in what follows, indicate that the locus ceruleus (LC), a small nucleus situated bilaterally in the brain stem (in the anterior pons), and the central nervous system (CNS) norepinephrine system connected with it may play a dual contributing role (1) in "tuning" the neural centers and mechanisms that subserve the prerequisite cognitive processes; and (2) in energizing the signaling response mechanism.

This small nucleus contains norepinephrine (NE), and provides more than 70 percent of the total norepinephrine in the primate brain, and indirectly controls a large part of the peripheral sympathetic nervous system. The LC appears to be the most extensively projecting neuronal system in the central nervous system. In anesthetized or paralyzed rats, LC neurons are activated by somatosensory stimuli (painful and otherwise) applied to any part of the body; auditory, visual, and various other environmental stimuli have been shown to activate LC neurons in awake-behaving rats and monkeys. Information from most, maybe all, sensory systems appears to funnel to the LC, and the LC transmits information to extensive diverse regions of the rest of the central nervous system (to be further discussed in what follows). Interest in this CNS system is further heightened by the fact that there is a great deal of evidence to indicate that it probably plays a centrally important role in several kinds of clinical anxiety states, including that associated with the opiate withdrawal syndromes.

Literally hundreds, perhaps thousands, of scientists have contributed to what is known about this system. I will orient this brief and focused account first (and primarily) around the work of D. E. Redmond, Jr., and his coworkers (Y. H. Huang, G. K. Aghajanian, M. Davis, S. J. Grant, J. E. Leckman, D. S. Charney, M. S. Gold, J. W. Maas, and others). Redmond's work has the double value of being particularly germane to the issues in focus in this book and of brilliantly illuminating the immense power and range of modern basic and clinical neuroscientific methods. These methods are indeed capable of enabling deliberate, integrated experimental approaches utilizing single-cell studies, combined behavioral and neurophysiologic and pharmacologic studies on nonhuman primates, and finally, controlled drug trials in patients suffering from complex clinical disorders. In the account that follows, I have not tried to arrange the studies in strict chronological order, but rather have tried to arrange them to convey a "story."

In a series of studies on nonhuman primates (monkeys), Redmond and his coworkers demonstrated that electrical stimulation of the LC "increased the frequency of several behaviors quantitatively and induced changes in physiologic measures characteristic of fear or anxiety, whereas lesions decreased the same measurements" (Redmond 1982, p. 477). Further they showed that the drug piperoxan, which increases LC activity, had effects like those of electrical stimulation, whereas the drug clonidine, which reduces LC activity, had effects like those of destructive lesions. All of these findings strongly suggested an association between LC activity and anxious or fearful behavior.

Aghajanian (1982) in single-cell studies in LC neurons had demonstrated that clonidine and morphine have a net inhibitory effect on LC neurons but act via different receptors. Based on these data and on the observation that many of the symptoms of opiate withdrawal are the same as those of sustained acute anxiety, Redmond along with coworkers (Gold and Kleber) conducted an initial clinical trial of clonidine for the treatment of acute opiate withdrawal symptoms in methadone-maintenance patients (Gold et al. 1978). They showed that a treatment of one to two weeks can lead to complete detoxification of addicts and recovery from the drug-dependent state without withdrawal symptoms.

The original clinical studies were replicated by Washton and Resnick (1980). Further clinical work by Gold, Kleber, Redmond, and other colleagues, has confirmed the original finding in both single- and double-blind studies, and the clinical methods and treatment protocols have been and continue to be further refined and developed.

Coincidentally, it is interesting and important to note that the clinical trial of clonidine, originally stimulated by studies of the single cell, in turn stimulated new basic science experiments. Aghajanian (1982) summarized his conclusions from these subsequent studies:

It can be concluded that opiates and alpha-2 agonists act via independent receptors within the LC to produce their similar depressant effects on net LC cell activity. . . . Alpha-adrenoceptors can mediate inhibitory actions of NE via recurrent axon collaterals. Epinephrine (E) inputs to LC cells (Fuxe et al., 1974) are also channeled through inhibitory alpha-2 adrenoceptors (Cedarbaum & Aghajanian, 1976). Inhibitory enkephalin (ENK) inputs are depicted as acting through a separate, opiate (OP) receptor. Thus, both alpha-2 adrenoceptors and opiate receptors are in a position to throttle the output of LC neurons when they are driven by various excitatory inputs. The similarities between the effects of opiates and alpha-2 agonists on LC neuronal firing lend credence to the concept that the alpha-2 agonist clonidine might suppress certain symptoms of opiate withdrawal by means of a parallel but independent action on LC cell activity (Pepper & Henderson, 1980). This therapy avoids a perpetuation of the opiate-dependent state by virtue of the fact that clonidine acts on a non-opiate receptor (p. 22).

What about extension of these studies to anxiety? Redmond (1982) concluded that the effects of piperoxan (an alpha-adrenergic antagonist), which increases LC activity, and the effects of clonidine, which suppresses it, are probably mediated by specific clonidine-binding receptor sites characterized neurophysiologically as alpha-2 adrenoceptors.

Redmond considers the behavioral data from primates to be consistent with presumed specific functions of the human neuroanatomic connections of the LC. These data suggest the LC might serve as a relay center for an "alarm" system, inducing "normal" fear or anxiety (during higher levels of activation). As we have already noted, the LC receives innervation directly from pain pathways throughout the body, and the LC shows sustained responses to repeated presentations of "noxious" stimuli even in anesthetized animals (Cedarbaum and Aghajanian 1978). The awake monkey rapidly habituates LC activity in response to novel non-noxious stimuli and demonstrates a consistent association of spontaneous LC activity with the level of "vigilance" and arousal (Foote et al. 1980). "Efferent pathways from the LC include most of the areas responsible for the physiological responses to pain and fear" (Redmond 1982, p. 477). In addition, there are pathways to and from the cerebral cortex which provide feedback loops that explain the apparent influence that the meaning or relevance of a stimulus may exercise on the response. These same feedback loops provide access to areas that may underlie the cognitive experience of the emotional state (or states) (Redmond 1977).

Redmond concludes,

> This circuitry therefore provides an outline of how the LC (perhaps in concert with other central noradrenergic nuclei) may function as a part of an alarm-relay system which modulates the disagreeable and emotional side of the response to pain. Such a system is also the logical one to have provided the evolutionary mechanism for elaboration of the anticipation of possible pain, into the emotions generally called fear or anxiety, as theorized in different ways both by Pavlov and by Freud (1982, p. 477).

The picture that emerges experimentally in the nonhuman primate is that of the LC functioning as an alarm system, filtering and discriminating relevant (potentially noxious) from irrelevant stimuli. Experientially induced high-intensity activation affects nearly every major brain and autonomic function that is activated by fear and exerts profound effects on behavior (Redmond 1977, 1979; Redmond and Huang 1979).

If 'normal' anxiety results, *in part,* from overactivity of brain LC-NA [NE] systems, then pathological or morbid anxiety might also be due to some longer lasting dysregulation of brain NA [NE] neurons leading to chronic functional overactivity, hypersensitive target neurons, or to an increased sensitivity of the LC to stimuli that signal impending physical or psychic pain. At the neuronal and molecular level this 'neuropathology' might consist of increases in neurotransmitter synthesis rate, neuronal firing rate, pre-synaptic release, post-synaptic receptor sensitivity, or decreases in neurotransmitter catabolism, reuptake, or 'auto-receptor' sensitivity (Redmond 1982, p. 477).

But this is not the whole story—it is yet to be fully evolved. Note that Redmond states that normal anxiety may result *"in part"* from overactivity of brain LC-NE systems. Other neurotransmitter systems are also implicated. The alpha-2 receptors also mediate indirectly some inhibitory reactions of imipramine, desmethylimipramine, and monoamine oxidase inhibitors—all three belonging to classes of drugs that are clinically effective in treatment of depression. Furthermore, other types of receptors in the same locations suppress LC firing and NE release or both—presumably via opiod or enkephalin neurotransmitters. Gamma amino butyric acid (GABA) receptors also seem to be located on LC cells and are thought to be involved in the modulating effect that benzodiazopines exert on LC cell activity (and anxiety), the latter effect brought about by an interaction of GABA and benzodiazopine receptors. The point I want to emphasize here is the role of multiple neurotransmitter systems, rather than of any single one, in the reactions. Perhaps they interact in intimate, reciprocal, but as yet unidentified ways in regulating and modulating this relay-alarm system.

Floyd E. Bloom and his coworkers (including S. C. Foote, G. Aston-Jones, G. F. Kolb, and others) do not visualize the LC-NE system as functioning only or mainly by excitatory effects. They emphasize the fact that the LC-NE system sends terminals widely throughout the CNS to end on both activating and inhibiting cells—and hence serves a very global function, enhancing whatever the target cells ordinarily do (whether it be stimulation or inhibition). These authors emphasize also that the LC cells may be influenced by two different input systems: one excitatory, reacting to salient external stimuli, the other inhibitory, reflecting internally generated signals in reaction to internal tonic vegetative requirements. This group of investigators has conducted extensive studies on unanesthetized (behaving) rats and squirrel monkeys. Collectively these studies have led them to regard the LC-NE system as a gating system that modulates as well as alarms—that works by differentially adjusting the "gain" of stimulating and inhibiting systems as CNS input is processed, thereby rendering the organism more or less responsive to the arousal strength of environmental stimuli. Thus, in some instances the system renders ordinarily neutral, innocuous stimuli anxiety provoking; in others it leads to absence of arousal in response to stimuli that ordinarily would or should generate alarm. In a forthcoming publication Aston-Jones et al. (1984) state:

Thus, NE-LC discharge may be controlled by phasic, exogenously determined inputs as well as by tonic, endogenously controlled afferents. Such powerful gating suggests specific behavioral consequences of NE-LC activity. Our working hypothesis states that robust NE-LC output may suppress CNS processes which have minimal value in phasically coping with unexpected external events, and simultaneously enhance driven activity within systems primarily concerned with such immediate behavioral responses. Conversely, tonically reduced NE-LC discharge may enable endogenously generated brain programs which mediate tonic vegetative behaviors. . . . In this way, the NE-LC system may bias the global orientation of behavior between the external and internal environments. The NE-LC may play a role in arousal and affective disorders as a consequence of its involvement in determining the global orientation of brain processing and behavioral activity. Similarly, the NE-LC system may have pronounced effects on sleep, anxiety and nociception, local brain metabolism and blood flow, and selective attention, all as aspects of its more general function of influencing the overall mode of brain information processing and therefore the global orientation of behavior.

ANOTHER PROBE

Bear in mind that the LC-NE system has rich two-way communication with the association cortex and the limbic system —the systems where *meanings* of current sensory input are processed and brought into associational connection with memories of past events. Clearly it is involved in evaluating and reacting to danger. I am tempted here to think about another probe for intermediate concepts that could be of heuristic value in ultimately bridging the gap between the neurobiologic and psychoanalytic sides. "Tracking" this biological (LC-NE) system which is thought to play such an important part in tuning and modulating cognitive processes and in activating autonomic responses could carry us in a direction converging toward concepts suggested by the psychoanalytic theory of signal anxiety.

Responses to psychological and psychosocial stressors can be thought of as occurring in four stages:

1. Recognition and evaluation of danger
2. Transduction
3. Activation of CNS stress mechanisms
4. Pathophysiologic sequelae in organs and tissues

In keeping with such a scheme I should think that operation of the mechanisms for signaling danger (signal anxiety, as described in psychological terms and conceptualized in psychoanalytic theory; function of the LC-NE system as described in neurophysiologic terms) must occur in stage 2. The danger-signaling system could thus be conceptualized as interposed between stages 1 and 3, and overlapping with parts of each of them, that is, with late events in stage 1 (recognition and evaluation) and early events in stage 3 (physiologic CNS activation).* Such a conceptualization would permit data on one side of the intermediate conceptual template we seek (chapter 1) to "speak" to the psychoanalytic theory of signal anxiety and defense mechanisms; data on the other side would "speak" to both the neural substrates of cognition (recognition and evaluation) and the physiology of autonomic and neuroendocrine activation in CNS centers. The test of its heuristic value would be the capacity of such a conceptualization to generate empirically testable hypotheses—a reasonable challenge, it seems to me. In fact I did venture tentatively to propose some ways of confronting that challenge earlier (chapter 111, p. 139).

THE BRAIN AS AN ENDOCRINE ORGAN

It is important to note that the NE system, along with dopaminergic and serotonergic systems in the brain, is also involved in selectively stimulating and/or inhibiting hypophysiotropic nuclei of the hypothalamus, and thereby can influence production of anterior pituitary hormones, including those involved in stress response (for example, adrenocorticotropic hormone [ACTH]). Consideration of these functions brings us to the next step in the staging of these stress reactions. It takes

*Indeed, recent data indicate that discriminative neurons in the prefrontal association cortex are diversified and that certain of them play a specific role in mnemonic coding, for example, as demonstrated during performance of the delayed response task, a test of elemental memory function discussed in chapter 10 (Kojima and Goldman-Rakic 1984). Additionally recent studies in Goldman-Rakic's laboratory demonstrate that fibers originating in neurons of the dorsal prefrontal cortex project directly to the LC, suggesting that the prefrontal association cortex exerts direct influence on the LC and secondarily on monoaminergic (NE) innervation of large areas of cerebral cortex (Arnsten and Goldman-Rakic, in press).

place in the hypothalamus. Neural circuits in the hypothalamus control and regulate vital body functions via autonomic, endocrine, and immune systems, and influence behavior through neural connections to higher cognitive centers and to systems concerned with drive and motivation. Higher cortical centers communicate with the hypothalamus via the limbic system; and the circuits making up the extensive bidirectional frontal-limbic-hypothalamic network of connections provide the anatomical pathways whereby emotions can reach consciousness and, conversely, whereby cognitive processes can influence emotional life.

Both input to and output from the hypothalamus utilize humoral as well as neural mechanisms, and in all possible neurohumoral combinations of input and output. One of the most important functions of the hypothalamus is contained in the capacity of certain neurons to serve both as nerve cells receiving and transmitting electrical information *and* as endocrine cells releasing substances into local and/or general circulation to act on nearby and/or distant structures. In other words, these neurons transduce neural information into hormonal information, which can then act at great distances, that is, on structures beyond the reach of nerve terminals. For example, the information can act on receptors located on lymphocytes, thereby influencing one aspect of immune processes. The many implications for clinical medicine seem clear.

But there is more to add to this part of the story that is even more interesting. One of the structures which is not out of reach of nerve terminals, and not at a long distance from the brain, nonetheless may be and often in fact is the target of "distant" humoral transmission. *It is the brain itself* (!), which can be the target of "neural-humoral-humoral" long feedback loops that originate in the brain. In such a reaction the information would go the long way around (see figure 12.1).

I am referring here to feedback loops such as those that involve hormones (secreted by peripheral endocrine glands) which act upon central monoamine systems in the brain stem. The latter, in turn, participate in central regulation of secretion of tropic hormones of the anterior pituitary—hormones which

153

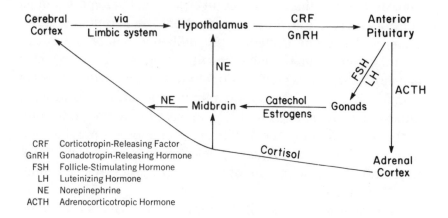

FIGURE 12.1

Feedback Loops: The Brain as a Target of Its Own Stress-Induced Responses

in turn are responsible for stimulating peripheral production of the very hormones that play back on the central mechanism. For example, cortisol and catecholestrogens produced by adrenal cortex and gonads (under influence of anterior pituitary tropic hormones) influence brain stem enzymes that regulate rates of synthesis and breakdown of monoamine (norepinephrine and dopamine) neurotransmitters in the brain that act to release the hypophysiotropic hormones that participated in production of cortisol and catecholestrogen in the first place. (See figure 12.1.)

There is still more information that is of interest in contemplating the mind-body issues under discussion. It comes from the new and rapidly expanding body of knowledge about peptides which are located in and active in the brain (Snyder 1980). Here I will refer specifically and mainly to one aspect of peptidergic hypothalamic and pituitary function under conditions of stress. Peptide neurohormones and their precursor peptides are synthesized in the cell bodies of the peptidergic neurons. Then they form into neurosecretory vesicles, which migrate down the axon to the nerve terminals for storage until released (secreted) when the neuronal cell body is appropriately stimulated. ACTH is known to be formed from a larger polypeptide, pro-opio-melanocortin, which as the name suggests, can be split by the action of specific enzymes acting at appropriate bonds to form three separate compounds—ACTH, melanocyte-stimulating hormone (MSH), and an opiod molecule (beta endorphin). That, in fact, is what does happen when corticotropin-releasing factor (CRF), secreted as a response to stress, acts on the larger prohormone polypeptide.

The larger precursor prohormone is found both in secretory cells of the anterior pituitary, where CRF reaches it via the portal circulation, and in the hypothalamus itself, where it is more directly accessible to CRF. Both MSH and beta endorphin acting directly in the brain have behavioral effects (e.g., MSH affects learning), whereas ACTH stimulates production of glucocorticoids by the adrenal cortex and these have mainly systemic metabolic effects. Since ACTH does not pass the blood brain barrier, when the reaction occurs in hypothalamus (on the brain side) the results can be expected to reflect mainly on CNS behavioral rather than systemic effects, that is, effects of MSH and beta endorphin. When breakdown of pro-opio-melanocortin takes place in the anterior pituitary on the other side of the blood brain barrier, systemic glucocorticoid effects (on electrolyte balance, carbohydrate metabolism, and so forth) can be expected to predominate. Factors determining where the reaction occurs have still not, to my knowledge, been finally demonstrated; but one factor that is involved as part of the process (i.e., the induction of the enzymes responsible for separating biologically active segments from the larger molecule) may well turn out to be regulated by genes.

Some other peptides originating in hypothalamic peptidergic neurons are released elsewhere in the brain (via axons that innervate areas of limbic structures) where they act as neurotransmitters in synaptic clefts. In this way, they may modulate neuron excitability and synaptic effectiveness in brain regions known to be involved in learning, modulation of mood, and various motivational states and appetitive behaviors (for example, cholecystokinin influences eating behavior).

Clearly the brain functions as the largest endocrine organ of the body.

To return to the task at hand, there are three nuclear cell groups in the hypothalamus that are of importance in regulating and/or influencing physiologic processes throughout the body including the brain. They are:

1. The head nuclei of the autonomic nervous system from which efferent pathways transverse brain stem, spinal cord, and peripheral autonomic ganglia to innervate tissues and organs.

2. The neuroendocrine peptidergic nuclei. Some neuroendocrine peptidergic cells secrete hypophysiotropic hormones in response to appropriate stimulation by various peptides and biogenic amines such as dopamine. The hypophysiotropic hormones or releasing factors (e.g., CRF) traverse the blood vessels of the local portal circulation surrounding the pituitary stalk and stimulate the anterior pituitary to secrete two kinds of hormones. First, the anterior pituitary secretes tropic hormones such as adrenocorticotropic and thyrotropic hormones which stimulate endocrine glands to secrete their products such as cortisol and thyroxine into the circulation, and, second, it also secretes hormones such as prolactin and somatostatin that act directly on peripheral tissue. Other peptidergic neuroendocrine cells of the hypothalamus secrete peptides directly into the systemic circulation by way of the posterior pituitary stalk (e.g., vasopressin and oxytocin). These peptides act as hormones stimulating receptors on distant cells, for example, on cells of the collecting ducts and convoluted tubules of the kidney.

3. The nuclear cells that influence function (competence) of the immune systems of the body (both cellular and humoral) indirectly via neuroendocrine and directly via neuroimmunologic mechanisms and pathways.

Implications for Clinical Medicine and Psychiatry

Consideration of the ways in which these systems of the hypothalamus respond to stress leads into a more clinically oriented discussion of the influence of stress on bodily and mental functions. That subject will be the theme of the next part of this book—it is what lies ahead as we approach from the neurobiologic side. But the questions will be different. They will be posed at a clinical rather than theoretical level. Splitting hairs, we could say that the questions are no longer mind-brain questions, but rather brain-body questions. We can assume (since it does happen) that somehow stressful, deeply personal meanings are processed cognitively somewhere in cortical-limbic-hypothalamic circuits, tuned and modulated by the LC-NE system, and so transduced to activate the hypothalamic nuclear cell groups listed earlier. The questions now will be:

1. What determines whether there will be clinically important consequences following stress?
2. If they occur, what are the mediating mechanisms?
3. If there are clinical sequelae, what forms will they take?

We've reached the clinical (formerly it might have been called the "psychosomatic") part of the book. The model that will be developed will regard at least some of the major "functional" psychoses as stress disorders with the brain as the target organ—and, if valid, will render distinction between "psychiatric," "psychosomatic," and "medical" disorders meaningless and out of date.

Part IV

BODY

IMPLICATIONS FOR CLINICAL MEDICINE AND PSYCHIATRY

CHAPTER 13

Psychophysiology of Stress and Its Clinical Sequelae

Introductory Orienting Ideas

STATES OF HEALTH and illness can be understood fully only in terms of all three of their relevant parameters: biological, psychological, and social. Each individual person can be regarded as a system, on the one hand comprised of subsystems and on the other constituting part of a larger environmental suprasystem. The "whole" is thus a superordinate open system, that is, one that allows free transactional interchanges of energy and information across boundaries. Although energy and information can flow freely in both directions between the person and his environment, the total energy level in the living person is higher than that of the surrounding environment (negative entropy). This is what it means biologically to be alive. When life ceases, the energy differential disappears.

Familiar concepts in psychology, the social sciences, and physiology fit comfortably into such a scheme. In psychology, "mind" constitutes the psychological subsystem of the person that articulates and interacts with meanings in the environment, such as symbols.

In the social sciences, "persons" are part of social groups or suprasystems—dyads, families, institutions, states, nations, cultures. When a person falls ill, new dyads and groups form and become important—the doctor-patient relationship, the patient-ward staff relationships, the doctor-patient-ward staff-hospital system-health care system relationships, and so forth. Transactions involve information (communication of meaning), matter and energy (such as the exchange or giving of money, food, or medications).

In physiology, organ systems, individual organs, tissues, cells, and subcellular elements constitute subsystems regulated by homeostatic mechanisms that are geared to maintain a constant internal environment in the face of external environmental challenges, or stresses. These mechanisms are in turn regulated in the central nervous system by (psychosomatic and somatopsychic) autonomic and neuroendocrine mechanisms. These latter mechanisms, in responding to meaningful external informational input and/or to conflictual intrapsychic meanings, generate emotions. Emotions, as noted earlier, combine psychological and physiologic features.

Developments in the field of neurobiology have only recently forced belated recognition that the brain is part of the body. This fact was largely overlooked in the early days of "psychosomatic medicine," when many investigators took it for granted that the "black box" (i.e., the brain) contained terminals and circuits wired in series so as to permit transmission more or less directly from one end of the box to the other: input (meaning) → affect → output (physiologic discharge). (See figure 13.1.) Many early theories in psychosomatic medicine relied heavily on postulated relationships between conflictual psychological content, physiologic concomitants of unresolved conflict, and pathophysiology of disease. In the spirit of the biomedical model and of Koch's postulates, early workers con-

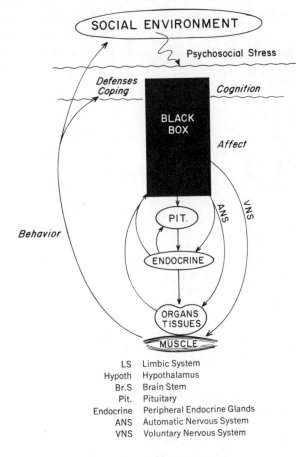

LS   Limbic System
Hypoth   Hypothalamus
Br.S   Brain Stem
Pit.   Pituitary
Endocrine   Peripheral Endocrine Glands
ANS   Automatic Nervous System
VNS   Voluntary Nervous System

FIGURE 13.1
Second Model of a Person in a Biopsychosocial Environment

centrated on a (then) understandable search for pathogenic psychological specificity, analogous to pathogenic bacterial specificity. The central focus was on the question of whether or not specific psychological factors constitute necessary and/ or sufficient factors in determining choice of organ system and disease. (For more appreciative and comprehensive reviews of this important and productive epoch of research in psychosomatic medicine, see Reiser 1975 and Weiner 1977.) The comments here do not do justice to this phase in the development of the field. Much of the original data is still valid and valuable

—it is the theoretical formulations that need to be reworked in the light of more recent developments. Identification of psychological factors that may influence choice of disease is still a valid and relevant issue, but how different it looks now in the context of modern neurobiology (see figure 13.2).

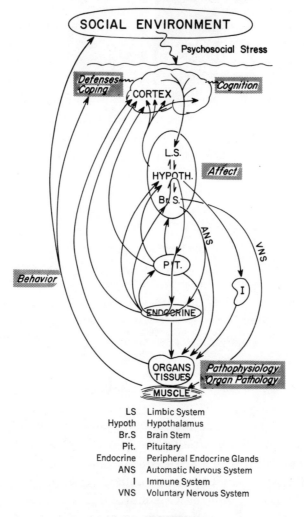

LS	Limbic System
Hypoth	Hypothalamus
Br.S	Brain Stem
Pit.	Pituitary
Endocrine	Peripheral Endocrine Glands
ANS	Automatic Nervous System
I	Immune System
VNS	Voluntary Nervous System

FIGURE 13.2

Third Model of a Person in a Biopsychosocial Environment

SOURCE: Reprinted with modification from "The Psychophysiology of Stress," *Stress and Coping,* Report No. 1. © 1980 by Smith Kline & French Laboratories. By permission of the publisher.

We focus now on the brain as central to understanding the person in illness and in health, recognizing:

1. That the brain functions to receive, process, evaluate, regulate, and store information and energy as they flow in both directions (and are at points transduced) along the society-mind-brain-body continuum;
2. That the brain simultaneously subserves and coordinates mental functions and behavior, via physiologic processes that regulate bodily functions (e.g., homeostatic and immunologic mechanisms); that these processes in turn influence tissue receptivity or resistance to pathogenic vectors of all types;
3. That the brain provides a common nexus of pathways and circuits that can serve as conduits for connecting both physiochemical and meaningful aspects of the environment with corresponding physiochemical and meaningful (psychological) aspects of the person;
4. That right and left hemispheres may to a surprising degree function autonomously and with different operational patterns, which generate very different modes of cognitive and affective functions which are of potential clinical interest;
5. That the dazzling complex of functions that have been listed here undergoes an epigenetic developmental evolution, initially programmed by genic instructions and subsequently molded—often in profound ways—by experience, especially in early life but to appreciable degrees throughout the entire life cycle.

Psychoneuropharmacologic along with psychoneuroendocrinologic and psychoneuroimmunologic studies indicate how hypothalamic nuclei—connected as they are with cerebral cortex, where meanings are processed, and with limbic system and brain stem structures, where affects are processed—could (some of them by activating efferent autonomic pathways, some by secreting hypophysiotropic hormones) participate in transducing nonphysical symbolic stimuli into physical (physiologic, electrochemical, and humoral) events in the brain and so lead to changes in function of body tissues. And in the opposite direction these studies indicate how metabolic endocrine and neurotransmitter pathways could be involved in transducing physical changes in the body into pyschophysiologic phenomena such as moods and even into nonphysical, psychological phenomena such as mental meanings. The data indicate how such things *could* happen, not actually how they *do* happen.

Clinical Psychophysiology of Stress, Part 1

The clinical psychophysiology of stress provides a logical stepping-off point for beginning the discussion of clinical and theoretical implications of ideas presented in chapters 1–12. In order to induce a clinically oriented mental set in readers (and at the same time provide a vivid reminder of the contrast between earlier and more recent literature) let me present a hypothetical multiple-choice question that might appear on a current certification or continuing medical education examination:

A 42-year-old type-A executive has recently been transferred to a new city. After working against overwhelming odds and a pressing deadline to gain an important new contract, he learns that he has lost it. Shortly afterward, he is passed over for the promotion he had hoped for when he was transferred. As he starts work on a new project, he develops which of the following? (*a*) myocardial infarction, (*b*) bleeding duodenal ulcer, (*c*) influenza complicated by pneumococcal pneumonia, (*d*) psychotic depression, (*e*) paranoid psychosis, (*f*) a phobia, (*g*) alcohol-dependent behavior (growing out of a previous social drinking pattern), (*h*) carcinoma of the colon, (*i*) midlife crisis with acting out.

We realize now that the answer might be any or none of the above.

The questions then, as noted earlier, are: (1) What determines if and when, there will be clinical sequelae to stressful situations? (2) What are the mechanisms involved? (3) If there are sequelae, what forms will they take? Will they manifest themselves primarily in the somatic, cognitive, affective, or behavioral spheres, or in some combination?

With regard to the first question, "stress" is a term that can carry a variety of connotations. In the clinical context the question of whether there will be important consequences following "stress" can be conceptualized as a problem involving a balance of forces—between the adaptive demand ("stress") and the internal "work" ("strain") involved as the person attempts to deal with it. Naturally, from a clinical point of view, it is the internal strain that is pathogenic. The question, then, really should be restated: When does stress lead to clinically important internal strain; what kind and how much strain is required to result in clinical consequences?

From a psychological, psychosocial perspective, the stressful impact of an event depends on the meaning it has for the individual. Bearing this in mind, it becomes readily apparent that what is meaningful for one person may not be meaningful to another. Whether a situation is meaningful and potentially strain-producing depends, as discussed in earlier chapters, on two intrapsychic factors. The first is what the potential symbolic meaningful referents of the event are relative to central unresolved conflicts; this can only be understood in terms of the individual's personal past history. The second is the effectiveness of ego defenses and coping devices available to deal with intrapsychic conflict and with challenging environmental situations.

It is important also to recognize that the "stress potential" of an event can be powerfully aggravated or greatly diminished by social factors, such as the presence or absence of satisfactory social support systems—family, friends, organizations, community structure, and so forth. Also, the meaning of an event is shaped and therefore is to be understood in relation to social factors such as socioeconomic status, group values, and cultural traditions.

When a stressful situation for any one, or combination, of the above reasons carries deep and powerful meaning for the individual, the sequence of responses set into motion does not seem to follow simple linear all-or-none response paradigms with fixed thresholds. Rather, clinical responses to stress can be thought of as constituting a continuum, from relatively mild at one end to severely disruptive at the other. As stress continues and intensifies, clinical problems may develop as manifestations of multiple dynamic, fluctuating psychological and physiologic defensive and coping mechanisms that are responding excessively, inappropriately, and/or inadequately to stress. To give a few examples, excessive defensive use of projection might lead to a paranoid state; overresponse or poorly modulated response of circulatory changes that are part of the "fight-flight" response can result in vasomotor instability and vascular malfunctions; and excessive neuroendocrine response may contribute to untoward changes in metabolic systems. The majority of clinical situations we deal with in practice probably occur somewhere in the mid-range of the stress intensity spectrum. At the most severe end of the spectrum are responses that occur when defenses have collapsed entirely: panic states, acute psychotic decompensation, and even profound, life-threatening physiologic disturbances.

To summarize, the circuitry and apparatus depicted in figure 13.2 illustrate the pathways by which meaningful, potentially stressful psychological input can be processed in the cerebral cortex, activate limbic system, brain stem, and hypothalamus. The hypothalamus, in turn, regulates the autonomic nervous, immune, and neuroendocrine systems. Finally, the affected endocrine glands and body tissues influence higher initiating and regulating centers via feedback loops. The evidence points to the hypothalamus as the locus where final steps in transduction of psychological stress into physical physiologic events most probably occur.

All of the foregoing pathways and mechanisms to body as well as those back to brain have only recently been appreciated for their highly important role as *nonspecific* mediators of the wide variety of pathogenic processes and clinical morbidity that have with high frequency been observed to follow in the wake of emotionally stressful life events. These patterns and mechanisms are nonspecific in respect to the actual disease process that may develop, since they seem to act by altering tissue resistance to pathogenic vectors of all kinds.

Coding or instruction for laying down of these mediating circuits is contained in the genes. Ultimately, the actual functional patterns displayed by these circuits can be and are profoundly shaped during development by learning and experience. I think it is in these complex epigenetic developmental processes that answers to questions of (psychological) specificity may still be hidden.

Let's start with an ordered survey of the clinical sequelae of stress—what can happen in the body when defenses are strained and the hypothalamic stress mechanisms have been activated? The answers will be relatively straightforward at first but will rather quickly force us to confront perplexing, mysterious, intriguing, challenging, and unsolved mind-body questions.

Clinical Psychophysiology of Stress, Part 2: A Survey

Stress-related clinical disorders may be manifest in somatic, affective, cognitive, and behavioral realms.

SOMATIC DISORDERS

Somatic disorders occur in three overlapping subgroups: functional psychophysiologic disorders, diseases resulting from failure of body defenses against pathogenic vectors, and the so-called psychosomatic disorders.

Functional Psychophysiologic Disorders. These do not by themselves lead to structural tissue change. In these conditions, symptoms result from reversible changes in function in autonomically innervated organs or organ systems, changes induced as concomitants of emotional arousal and patterned as variants of the activation physiology of "fight or flight" originally described by Cannon (1915). Most reactions of this type are transient and have mainly "nuisance" value (for example, preexamination diarrhea, butterflies in the stomach); some may be symptomatically severe but not serious (for example, vasodepressor syncope); others by virtue of persistence or recurrence may in combination with other factors contribute to development of structural tissue change (for example, excessive perspiration may aggravate dermatologic conditions, constipation may contribute to development of diverticulitis). Finally, it is possible for some reactions of this type to eventuate in serious clinical events. For example, intense and sustained anxiety which, like exertion, creates a demand for increased work on heart muscle, may precipitate congestive heart failure or even fatal arrhythmia in patients susceptible because of underlying structure heart disease (Lown et al. 1980).

Diseases Resulting from Failure of Body Defenses Against Pathogenic Vectors. This second subclass of somatic disorders includes all varieties of disease in which there is a critical imbalance between (1) the strength or virulence of infecting organisms (or other pathogenic agents such as allergens and metastatic cancer cells) and (2) the strength of host resistance. This critical balance determines whether illness will occur or whether the body will successfully fight off the challenging pathogenic vector(s). Psychological and psychosocial factors exert vitally important influences on this balance, and hence on this whole class of diseases, through effects on host resisttance. As depicted in figure 13.2, there are four pathways whereby hypothalamic stress reactions may affect resistance or receptivity of tissue:

1. Via direct neural connections to organs through autonomic outflow paths
2. Via indirect psychoneuroendocrine mechanisms (hypothalamus → pituitary → tropic hormones → peripheral endocrine glands → hormones acting on tissue)
3. Via direct psychoneuroendocrine mechanisms (hypothalamus → pituitary → hormones that themselves act directly on body tissues, e.g., growth hormone, prolactin, oxytocin, vasopressin)
4. Via psychoneuroimmune and psychoneuroendocrine mechanisms that directly or indirectly respectively influence competence of immune systems

Psychoneuroimmunology is a relatively recent but rapidly progressing field which has already in fundamental ways widened and deepened our appreciation of the role of central nervous system in mediating psychosocial influences on health and disease. Comprehensive reviews of both experimental (animal) and clinical studies published by several of the field's leading investigators summarize and explicate the multiple ways in which the immune systems of the body may be regulated, modulated, and monitored by the brain (Solomon and Amkraut 1981; Stein et al. 1981).

Hypothalamic centers exert direct influences on cellular *and* humoral immune mechanisms (on T-cell and B-cell functions, respectively). The hypothalamus also exerts indirect influences on immune function through its control of the endocrine system and the production of its various hormones (particularly cortisol). R. Ader (1981) and colleagues have shown that immunosuppression can be classically conditioned. Rhythmic (circadian) fluctuations in immune competence are probably programmed centrally. M. Stein and colleagues have demonstrated changes indicative of decreased immune competence in widowers during time-specified epochs of bereavement (Schleifer et al. 1983). Thymic function is now known to be intimately involved along with the central nervous system in regulation of immune systems, although details of these latter interactions remain to be worked out. The immune system of the body and the central nervous system have been shown to be intimately involved with each other from earliest developmental stages on. Competence of the immune system and integration of its various components in adulthood have been shown to be dependent on early developmental experience. Such effects have been demonstrated in animals by experimental manipulations, for example, in handling and in housing conditions, during infancy.

The clinical literature extensively documents the role of emotional factors—especially failure of psychological defenses—in influencing time of onset and course of infectious and neoplastic diseases as well as of autoimmune and allergic disorders (see Solomon and Amkraut 1981).

But there is still more. In order to maintain optimal host resistance in tissues, all of the neural, psychoneuroendocrine, and psychoneuroimmune systems we have been discussing must be not only "orchestrated," or synchronized, but also harmoniously entrained to a variety of biorhythms. Environmentally paced biorhythms include the twenty-four-hour circadian rhythm, related to the rotation of the earth around the sun, which produces alternating periods of light and darkness; the twenty-eight-day infradian rhythm, related to the rotation of the moon around the earth; the three-month seasonal rhythm associated with spring, summer, autumn, and winter. And there is also the internally paced ultradian ninety-minute biorhythm manifested during sleep as recurrent "rapid eye movement" (REM sleep) periods.

Each of these biorhythms exerts (potentially separate) effects on the person's levels of rest and activity—on levels of activity of individual endocrine glands, on general metabolic systems, on immune systems, and on sensitivity of neuronal membrane receptors to agonist, antagonist, and modulatory substances at synaptic clefts (thereby influencing neurotransmitter systems). Synchronization of endogenously generated internal rhythms with each other and their entrainment with environmental rhythms is accomplished in the brain. It is not hard to understand how disruption and desynchronization of these systems can upset dynamic biological balances, nor should it be difficult to appreciate the important health-maintaining role of the physiologic and psychological mechanisms that have been developed during the course of evolution for dealing with stress. The wonder isn't only why and how we fall ill when we do but also how we manage to stay as well as we do most of the time.

All of the mechanisms we have reviewed so far are best regarded as nonspecific in respect to (choice of) disease. They are important in precipitating illness and in influencing the course of disease once established, but not in preprogramming within an individual the capacity to develop a specific disease. That issue arises when we approach the next subclass of somatic disorders, the "psychosomatic" disorders.

"Psychosomatic" Disorders. Why do individuals develop one disease rather than another? Do psychological factors play a role in processes that determine choice of illness? I can't

think of a more confusing word than "psychosomatic." I was tempted not to use it but realized that the issues raised by this class of diseases can't be made to go away by avoiding the word, which, in any case, is now long established by conventional use in the medical literature.

The issues that lead to considering anything beyond a nonspecific precipitating role for psychophysiologic mechanisms in etiology and pathogenesis arise in connection with diseases of unknown etiology. You have probably noticed that up to this point I have emphasized tissue resistance to specific insults: to infecting pathogenic organisms, to effects of trauma, to allergens, to metastatic implantation of invading malignant tumor cells and, I might even have added, to an activated oncogene in a parent tumor cell. In confronting diseases of unknown or incompletely understood etiology, it is quite natural to search for additional, unidentified or unproven factors that could be involved in etiology and pathogenesis, factors such as genetic abnormalities, degenerative processes, long-delayed effects of "slow" viruses, and unidentified toxins. It is in this connection that the question arose originally as to whether psychological factors might play a specific role. The story is at best muddled and incomplete. At first it looked as if they very well might; now it looks as if they might not—or, at least, if they play this role, in ways very different from those originally thought.

As promised, I won't attempt a comprehensive review of psychosomatic literature. What I propose instead is to cull from it, and share with you, data that have led me to think seriously about preprogrammed brain circuits and even to speculate about the role that experience and learning might play in influencing development of genetically "designed" brain circuits that govern psychophysiologic responses and bodily reactions to stress. But, that is getting ahead of the story —first, some historical background.

Beginning around 1940, many investigators from a variety of disciplines, especially psychiatrists, psychoanalysts, internists, clinical psychologists, and psychophysiologists, undertook extensive combined medical and psychiatric studies of patients with chronic diseases of unknown etiology. Representative of such studies and perhaps the most enduringly influential were those conducted by a group under the leadership of Franz Alexander at the Chicago Psychoanalytic Institute (Alexander et al. 1968). Their research focused ultimately and mainly on seven diseases, which were to become regarded as the classic psychosomatic diseases (sometimes affectionately referred to as the "Chicago Big Seven"): essential hypertension, peptic duodenal ulcer, ulcerative colitis, thyrotoxicosis, neurodermatitis, rheumatoid arthritis, and bronchial asthma. This inventory was artifactual. It reflected logistics of investigator interest, energy, and time; levels of patient interest and availability; and the state of the art and knowledge base available—and it led to a narrow view of the field. Within the context of broader current biopsychosocial perspectives on health and illness (Engel 1977), the term "psychosomatic" denotes a multidisciplinary approach to clinical problems rather than a limited group of clinical disorders.

While early psychosomatic "specificity" theories, burdened by methodological and conceptual difficulties and by limitations of the biomedical data available, are no longer tenable (Reiser 1975), there are reliable data to be extracted from early studies that should be taken into account in new and/or revised theories. For example, when patients with and without various of the classic psychosomatic diseases were individually studied in psychological depth, and the findings then grouped and collated according to diagnosis, some interesting data emerged.

Groups of patients with the same psychosomatic disease demonstrated shared psychological characteristics such as personality structure, nature of core unresolved conflicts, types of defense mechanisms characteristically employed, and the types of psychosocial situations apt to activate the core conflicts and to be associated with precipitation and/or exacerbation of the illness. *And* the extent of sharing (that is, of psychological overlap) displayed between patients with the same classic psychosomatic disease was greater than the extent of sharing between them and patients with other diseases. For example, patients with peptic duodenal ulcer more resembled each other in respect to the psychological characteristics listed above than they resembled patients with other diseases (rheumatic valvular heart disease, for example). Psychologically they were "sisters under the skin," so to speak.

Such resemblances, however, could be explained by the fact that patients with the same disease share the same illness experiences, worries, symptoms, medications, dietary regimens, limitations of activity, and so forth. Their shared psychological characteristics, then, could very well represent reactions to shared basic illness experiences. There is no way to rule out such a somatopsychic basis for the resemblance when the patients have been studied retrospectively, that is, after the disease has already developed.

But what if healthy persons were to be studied before becoming ill, that is, prospectively? It is possible and practically feasible to do a prospective study when there is a biological marker that will identify healthy persons who are "at risk," that is, capable of developing the disease in question and likely to do so if appropriately stressed or otherwise stimulated. In such a prospective study, correlations between the presence of defined psychological characteristics and presence of a known biological marker for the disease would antedate the active illness. The psychological traits could then be regarded as correlates or counterparts in the psychological realm of the marker trait in the biological realm.

There are such studies. The clearest one to date in the psychosomatic area (Weiner et al. 1957) prospectively correlated psychological traits characteristic of peptic duodenal ulcer patients with the biological trait that marks the capacity to develop peptic duodenal ulcer even before it develops (high level of serum pepsinogen). In this study psychological and biological data were processed "blind"; data were coded so that those who worked on the data of the psychological tests and clinical interviews did not know the results of the biological assays, which were carried out by a separate research group in a different laboratory. The total group of subjects consisted of 2,073 randomly chosen draftees at an army induction center. All were classified according to serum pepsinogen level—and all were initially administered preliminary psychological screening tests. A subsample (experimental group) of 120 (63 hypersecretors and 57 hyposecretors) were selected for special psychological study, consisting of a battery of projective psychological tests and a clinical interview. And each of this subsample was given a complete gastrointestinal roentgen examination before being sent to a sixteen-week basic training experience—which served as a real life psychosocial stress situation.

All but 13 of the subsample were again given the psychological tests and roentogenologic examinations some time between the middle and end of the basic training period. As with the biochemical tests, the findings of these examinations were not available to the psychological researchers until the study had been completed. The first roentgenologic examinations revealed evidence of healed duodenal ulcers in 3 and an active ulcer in one of the 63 men with pepsinogen hypersecretion. The second roentgenologic examination revealed evidence of active duodenal ulcers in an additional 5 men who had no evidence of such lesions at the beginning of the study. All subjects who had or developed evidence of duodenal ulcer were among the 63 with high blood pepsinogen values.

Psychological data, processed independently as already noted and using primarily Alexander's formulations of the core conflicts he considered specific for patients with peptic ulcer, identified 10 men of the experimental subgroup of 120 as most likely to develop an ulcer. Not only did their test material correspond to Alexander's psychological descriptions and formulations about patients with peptic ulcer but these men also showed evidence of current intense activation of the core conflicts. The predictions were accurate in 7 out of the 10 cases. Of the 3 men who did not have or did not develop an ulcer, 2 were hypersecretors. Of the 10 selected as candidates, then, 9 were hypersecretors.

In the same study we examined the independent psychological test data gathered on the 111 patients of the experimental subgroup who did not have or develop peptic ulcer in connection with the stress of military induction and basic training (54 with high pepsinogen and 57 with low pepsinogen levels). Those with the high values differed significantly from those with the low values, again showing more of the characteristics formulated by Alexander as specific for peptic ulcer, but not with the same intensity as those who did actually demonstrate lesions. As noted earlier, intensity of the activated core conflicts turned out to be the additional element predictive of those who demonstrated actual ulcers on roentgen examination.

Here, then, is a powerful residue of data that remains to be explained: patients with peptic duodenal ulcer showed greater psychological resemblance to one another *and* to healthy subjects with the (genetically determined) biological trait marker for duodenal ulcer (high serum pepsinogen) than they did to patients with other diseases or to healthy subjects without the biological trait marker. Similar findings of specific psychological intragroup resemblances being greater than intergroup resemblances have also turned up in studies of patients with other classic psychosomatic diseases (thyrotoxicosis, some forms of rheumatoid arthritis, and some forms of essential hypertension). And there are for those conditions similar suggestive, but not comparably definitive, prospective findings. (Comparably precise biological markers that would render such studies more feasible have not yet been identified).

I've presented the "best case" to make a single point: Such findings strongly support the idea that individuals may show evidence of the predisposition in both the psychological and the physiologic realms even before the disease has developed; and the fact that the psychological characteristics demonstrable in vulnerable persons beforehand are comparable to those displayed by patients with active disease strongly suggests that there must be a meaningful relationship between predictive premorbid psychological and biological traits.

Clearly the possibility exists that there may be a group of diseases (now called psychosomatic) in which psychological and psychosocial factors play more than a precipitating or facilitating role in pathogenesis (see also Alexander et al. 1968). I would like to return now to completing the clinical survey and to postpone further, and more speculative, discussion of the theoretical implications until the final chapter.

COGNITIVE AND AFFECTIVE DISORDERS

It is clear from a vast clinical and basic psychoneuropharmacologic literature that dysfunctions of brain neurotransmitter systems are somehow centrally involved in the pathogenesis of at least two major classes of psychiatric disorders: (1) those presenting clinically as disturbances mainly of affect (unipolar depression, bipolar manic-depressive disorders, and a variety of severe anxiety and panic states), and (2) those presenting clinically as disturbances mainly of cognitive processes (the schizophrenias).

In both of these classes of psychiatric disorder (affective and cognitive), centrally acting pharmacologic agents that affect the function of neurotransmitter systems may exert profound effects on the symptoms and clinical course of patients—strong enough even to have enabled major changes to have been made in patterns and principles of clinical care and management. But our understanding is still far from complete. It is true that some of the symptomatic effects of drugs with known actions indicate the existence of rather specific neurophysiologic-behavioral correlations (dopaminergic systems with certain symptoms of schizophrenia; acetylcholine, norepinephrine, and serotonin systems with symptoms of affective disorders; norepinephrine, endorphin, and gamma amino butyric acid systems with symptoms of some anxiety, panic, and drug-withdrawal states). Nonetheless, the pharmacologic agents do not cure the underlying disorders, but rather aid in controlling them—similar perhaps to the role of insulin in diabetes. Many questions remain concerning etiology and precise details of pathogenesis.

Even so we do know that dysfunctions of neurotransmitter systems are intimately involved in these clinical disorders, and we do know that these same systems are intimately involved in the psychoneuroendocrine stress circuits. In fact, they occupy a crucial, centrally placed position in the feedback circuits that start in higher cortical centers (where meanings are processed) and pass down through all levels of brain to peripheral endocrine glands and tissues, with feedback loops returning to virtually all levels of brain from virtually all levels of the peripheral circuits (see figures 12.1 and 13.2). In my view, these facts constitute sufficient justification for raising the possibility that these clinical disorders may be stress diseases in which the brain is the "target organ"—an idea I've already mentioned and would now like to spell out more fully.

As in the case of all diseases of unknown etiology (including "psychosomatic" diseases) whose natural courses are marked by variable age of onset, remissions, and exacerbations, cognitive and affective disorders confront us with two major questions:

1. Why and how does the patient fall ill at a specific time?
2. Why does the patient fall ill with a particular disease rather than any one of all the others to which the human organism is prey?

My response to the first question can easily be anticipated from all that has gone before: one circumstance in which the patient can be expected to fall ill would be when confronted by a stressful situation which overwhelms defenses and coping mechanisms and so activates neuroendocrine and neuroimmune stress circuits and systems. If the stress is psychological and/or psychosocial, then the challenge would consist of the conflictful meanings it presents and the failed "first-line" defenses would be psychological defense mechanisms and coping behaviors.

I want to emphasize three points here. The first is that stress may be only one circumstance for precipitating or inducing an initial or recurring episode of illness. In some patients these events may be entrained or built-in (endogenous oscillator) mechanisms, as, for example, occurs in patients with precisely cycled alternating episodes of mania and depression. But such patients do not constitute the majority of those encountered in the clinic. I do not think we really know how many irregularly spaced episodes of major psychiatric illness are basically "endogenous." This leads to the second point, namely, that the ideational content of pathogenic psychological conflict is usually not present in or readily accessible to the patient's consciousness and the patient may be quite unaware of being in a situation of special personal psychological or psychosocial stress. Often it requires careful inquiry into life circumstances and events, and evaluation of their meaning against the background of the patient's personal history, to be reasonably certain about the absence of psychological stress. I wonder how many episodes of psychiatric illness (e.g., depression) recorded as "endogenous" are truly without meaningful precipitating event.

No matter, in this context it is not a central issue. For the majority of episodes of illness that *are* clearly precipitated by psychological psychosocial stress, the issue I wish to emphasize here is that the process begins at the level of *meaning,* that is, in the psychological realm and that, as already noted many times, somewhere, somehow these stimuli, which are themselves without physical properties, must be transduced into the physical realm. The fact that the clinical manifestations may be so profoundly influenced by drugs does not mean that the disorder is primarily and entirely "organic" or "biochemical"; it clearly does not justify patently incomplete conceptualizations of psychiatric illness—conceptualizations that fail to include mental processes (the realm of meanings, of subjective mental distress, and of conflicted motives). This merges into the third point. It is that once an aberrant or pathogenic physiologic function—for instance, increased rate of reuptake of norepinephrine from the synaptic cleft—has been set in motion, this physiologic process, even though it may have been initiated by a chain of reactions that started with a set of meanings conveyed to the patient in language, may now be beyond the reach of words. To put it another way, an ongoing metabolic process, once started by whatever stimuli, may be self-sustaining and run its course without being subject to influence by psychological vectors alone.

This point has important implications for conceptualizing the role of psychotherapy with a patient during a psychotic episode. A drug or physical mode of treatment and a therapeutic milieu may well be required to deal optimally with the disordered metabolic process and the disordered behavior. Individual psychotherapy would be supportive and adjunctive during this phase, with the place of insight and verbal clarification then coming into its own, so to speak, after brain metabolism and the patient's behavior had been restored to a more normal mode. The role of subsequent psychotherapy in appropriate instances would be to help the patient understand the meaning of what had transpired during the episode and what it was that had overwhelmed him, often including acquainting him with his unwitting complicity and participation in the development and generation of the stressful situation. The long-term goal would be to enable the patient, through understanding, to avoid repetition—to be able subsequently to deal with similar problems in different and, for him, less stressful ways. Comprehensive clinical management addresses all dimensions (biological, psychological, and social) insofar as is possible and feasible. The treatment regimen is programmed so as to take into account the phase of the illness; technical and modal priorities are adjusted over time as the patient's clinical course reflects a sequence of changing states of functional psychophysiologic balance.

I have in this section taken the liberty of grouping together a generic class or "family" of major psychiatric disorders related to one another by virtue of resting on neurotransmitter systems dysfunction. I realize this is a vague categorization but, given our present knowledge base, think it may be better that way. Although we know many details about separate transmitters, we are not sure yet how many there will ultimately turn out to be; nor do we have an organized or complete perspective on their functional interrelationships (synergistic and/or antagonistic actions), on their ontogenetic development, on shared functional redundancies, or on clinically significant exclusive functional features of individual molecules. In other words, we need to know more about how these systems are constituted, organized, and orchestrated in health and in conditions of disordered mental function. Each passing day brings surprises. For example, this "family" may be bigger than we thought. Depressive states, panic states, and agoraphobia may belong to this same family and be closer relatives than one would have thought. Panic states and chronic anxiety may be less closely related than we might have expected them to be.

The studies of Donald Klein and his colleagues, as well as other workers, illustrate the immense power of combining carefully controlled experimental studies of differential drug effects with careful clinical observations. Clinical anxiety states then turn out to be an unexpectedly heterogeneous group. For example, clinical responses to drugs suggest that some groups (such as patients with panic states, which respond to tricyclic antidepressants and MAO inhibitors but not to benzodiazepines) may be more closely aligned with depressions than others (such as patients with chronic anxiety states, which respond to benzodiazepines but not to tricyclic antidepressants). It is indeed intriguing that the analysis of Carol's panic attack in the subway and instant subway phobia (chapter 4) constitutes one instance in which an unexplained, apparently unprovoked, "spontaneous" panic attack turned out to be quite specifically instigated by revival of a conflicted core memory—connected with *separation from mother*.

Klein (1981) relates the core mechanisms of panic attacks to Bowlby's ethological concept of an evolved protest mechanism "with the evolutionary 'purpose' of causing the vulnerable infant to emit signals that will elicit retrieval by the mothering parent or by others" (Klein 1981, p. 247), a mechanism instinctively released by separation during the appropriate developmental phase. Klein prefers this to Freud's concept of signal anxiety evoked by an age-appropriate danger situation (threatened or impending loss of mother portending development of the traumatic situation of being overwhelmed by excitation in mother's absence). Interestingly, the theoretical distance between Bowlby's and Freud's ideas may not be all that great. Let me quote again Freud's own words (see also p. 89) about the infant's anxiety reaction to the absence of the mother: "This reaction is still an expedient one in the infant in arms, for the discharge, being directed into the respiratory and vocal muscular apparatus, now calls the mother to it, just as it activated the lungs of the new born baby to get rid of the internal stimuli" (Freud 1926, p. 137).

I do not raise this to argue about theoretical formulations. I agree with Klein when he says: "Naturalistic clinical observation remains one of our best sources of hypotheses, but clinical experimentation is the reality testing road to knowledge" (Klein 1981). Differences in theoretical interpretation are to be expected—they add spice to the research endeavor—and are in the long run unimportant as long as we are open to new facts and distinguish between knowledge and conceptualizations. Differential drug responses (observational data in one realm) do not really illuminate inner psychological experience (from a different realm) any more than the psychoanalytic elucidation of a patient's inner deep psychological experience illuminates the neuropharmacology of drug response. Facts are what they are. They do not change; theories should, can, and do change in response to new facts, which are uncovered by careful observation and experimentation and then subjected to rigorous logical analysis.

As discussed in chapter 10, it would be interesting to know what effect tricyclics, MAO inhibitors, and benzodiazepines would have had (or failed to have had) on Carol's anxiety symptoms. That information, if we had it, could be helpful in the search for neural mechanisms involved in generating her symptoms and perhaps could even bear indirectly on the nature of neural mechanisms connected with the memory functions involved. But I do not think that it alone would settle one way or the other the conceptual choice (if one feels a need to choose) between the Bowlby and Freud formulations.

BEHAVIORAL AND MIXED DISORDERS

Unresolved conflict that is held outside a person's awareness may be manifest in unwitting repetitive patterns of behavior that recurringly lead to situations that re-create earlier problems and traumatic situations. Carol's series of unfulfilling romantic involvements with eligible men—all of which came to the same end—are prototypical of this kind of behavioral disorder, of psychically determined behavior rooted in characterological psychopathology. (The same is true of Jim's job history, which is discussed in chapter 14). Stressful life situations that set up resonances in confictful memory networks and revive associated unpleasant affects and unwelcome motives may also lead to neurotically determined regressive defensive behaviors that usually, but not always, turn out to be (to varying degrees) inappropriate and ineffective.

As would be expected, there is always some admixture of disturbed behavioral manifestations in patients belonging to the other classes of clinical psychiatric disorders already discussed. Often these can be regarded as incidental, alternate, or additional ways of attempting conflict resolution. But in some instances they are more than incidental; that is, they become enmeshed in complex psychopathologic-psychologic-psychophysiologic processes. Some may even arise as reactions to the extreme discomfort of illness. The development of agoraphobic behavior and chronic anxiety states as reactions evolving in the wake of the intense psychic distress of panic attacks can serve as an example. In these instances the "secondary" condition (chronic anxiety state) may ultimately clinically overshadow the original panic condition; and the nature of the patient's drug responses may then give evidence that the underlying neurophysiological-neurochemical processes have also changed.

Anorexia nervosa can serve as an example of a differently constructed complex web. It is of particular interest because it underlines the importance of the social, societal influences, and the immense power of vectors in that sector to enter into the interactive psychological-biological processes that constitute the central focus of this volume. In anorexia nervosa the trouble seems to start (often precipitated by psychologically meaningful stress) with the development of complex mixtures of inappropriate behaviors and ideas associated with food and eating (anorexia, bulimia, self-induced vomiting, laxative overuse) and with physical activity, mainly excessive exercise, in order to control body weight. The latter concerns (exercise and body weight) are associated with disturbances of intrapsychic body image, sometimes of delusional proportion. The incidence of anorexia nervosa is increasing at such a rapid pace (in some socioeconomic sectors of the population it is reaching epidemic proportions) as to invoke the idea of "social contagion."

If the questions were limited to the psychological-sociological interrelationships involved, that would be enough! But, as everyone knows, the situation is far more complex. There are also major biological changes. In the wake of the disordered eating behavior, weight loss and malnutrition ensue, sometimes severe enough to cause death from intercurrent infection against which the immune systems of the malnourished body are ineffective. Menses and ovulation usually cease, and an altered circadian pattern of prolactin secretion may occur. The pattern of prolactin secretion in some patients with anorexia nervosa may follow a prepubertal pattern, and this can be regarded as a reflection of profound abnormalities in regulating hypothalamic pituitary neuroendocrine systems. Like the cognitive and affective disorders, even though precipitated often by psychological stress, the fully developed syndrome is therapeutically beyond the reach of words alone. Regardless of the vantage point from which you choose to view the problem, it certainly is not clear which is the cart and which is the horse. Or is that question even relevant?

In respect to this broad grouping of affective cognitive and behavioral disorders, the response to the second question (why a particular disease instead of all the other possible ones?) leads us to the same place we arrived in discussing "psychosomatic disorders." Specifically, we are led to the postulate that in the preclinical phase individuals may possess specific vulnerabilities in specific neurotransmitter systems and so be "at risk" for developing specific clinical syndromes in the wake of stress responses that are in themselves physiologically nonspecific in respect to disease.

CHAPTER 14

Jim, Another Clinical Example

FOR a number of reasons, this is a good juncture at which to present another clinical example, before embarking on a more theoretical final chapter. To begin with, preceding chapters have drawn on such a variety of (basic and clinical) disciplinary, conceptual, and methodological approaches as to render attempts at synthesis not merely difficult but in fact impossible. We knew this from the beginning. The search, rather, has been for a clinical perspective and for a useful way of approaching data from the two widely disparate realms of mind and brain —one without any physical qualities, the other with many.

The clinical report that follows has been abstracted from four years of psychoanalytic work (five hours per week). It has been abstracted in such a way as to focus on selected thematic contents, on interpretive formulations, reconstructions, and inferred meanings derived from the data provided by the psychoanalytic method. These formulated meanings constitute what this method was able to contribute toward understanding the psychological nature of the patient's symptoms and characterological symptomatic behaviors. Because some of Jim's symptoms also involved physiologic manifestations (premature ejaculation, severe anxiety, and sometimes panic states with spontaneous ejaculation), this case example also provides opportunity for using a dual-track approach to see what physiologic and neuropharmacologic approaches can contribute to understanding some of the physiologic aspects of his clinical psychophysiologic symptoms. As you will see, each track takes us a good part of the way *toward* but *not to* a point of convergence, and so in the end leaves us in the dark—a good illustration of the state of the art(s) as we venture further to probe the realm of theory.

Jim

Jim, a twenty-eight-year-old chemistry technician, came to psychoanalysis wanting help for a long-standing neurotic character disorder and for intractable premature ejaculation (despite many encounters, he had never satisfactorily completed sexual intercourse). He also suffered from panic states, sometimes associated with spontaneous (paradoxical) ejaculation without erection and without conscious sexual thoughts or feelings.

The work of his analysis enabled us to understand how each of these difficulties had roots in the protracted and intensely upsetting circumstances of his mother's long terminal illness and death from uterine cancer when he was five years old. The issue of separation from mother was at the core of an intricately tangled jumble of conflicts. She had been ill for a year and for the last six months of her life was unable to care for home and family (her husband, the patient, and a sister, who was two years older). At that time the home was broken up. Mother went to the hospital, Jim and his sister were sent to an institution (orphanage), and Father went to live with relatives.

At the beginning of his analysis, Jim told of frequent, regular visits with his father to his mother's sickroom in the hospital. When visiting hours were over, Mother, weeping and often out of control, would cling to him, wanting to delay the separation until the very last possible moment. Often, as Jim remembered it, he had to be forcibly pulled away from the clutch of her embrace. At the time of beginning analysis he mainly remembered—as you might well expect, considering that he was at the time a five-year-old boy—feeling uncomfortable, sometimes smothered, and always restless in her embrace, impatient and finally relieved to be freed from it and to leave the sickroom even though this meant being returned to the orphanage. Of course, there was a lot more to be remembered than that, and we did learn about it later; but it isn't difficult even with this preliminary information to begin to understand how such a scenario could provide background for some of Jim's later problems, if memories of it were to be revived and stirred into resonance during passionate sexual embraces.

But let's leave this theme for the time being and trace forward along another thematic track. After Mother's death, Jim and his sister remained in the orphanage for another two years. Though one wasn't supposed to like being in such a place, he remembered aspects he did like. The food was good, the atmosphere was calm, the rules were clear and made things predictable. (Father had a terrible temper and his house had always been stormy; there had been sudden temper outbursts, arguments between the parents, and frequently even physical abuse of the mother.) Jim learned to be well behaved and soon became the matron's favorite—the very model of a "good boy." Only one problem—enuresis—clouded that image; he feared he would fall from her favor if she knew. He went to great pains to change his bedclothes during the night and to hide them so she would not find the wet sheets on his bed and "know."

During these two years Jim longed for a mother and a home of his own. Often on Sundays couples interested in adopting would visit the home to look at children they might want to take. He wanted to be adopted, but was repeatedly rejected and felt disappointed not to be chosen.

Finally, Father took Jim and his sister to live with him, first at their aunt's house and then with two successive stepmothers. Father argued and fought with all of them. All of these women were remembered by Jim as being impatient, rigid, bad-natured, mean, and restrictive. All threatened to send him back to the orphanage whenever he didn't mind (not often) or if he wet the bed again (that persisted intermittently until age ten or eleven, but largely he was able to keep it under cover, so to speak). Being sent back to the orphanage always seemed the worst thing that could happen. (Later we learned that the conscious fear of being sent there was, as Freud taught, accompanied by an unconscious wish to be sent back. We'll get to that shortly.)

During all of this time, his memories of Mother became more idealized. Increasingly, he missed and longed for her, began to make up stories and fantasies about her, hopeful that she was still somewhere, watching over him. It is Jim's series of fantasy images of Mother, which began during this period, that I'd like to trace now.

1. While he was living with his father and aunt (latency period) his bedroom window faced the direction of a revolving beacon light. As he lay in bed waiting for sleep and the light rhythmically shone into his window, he imagined—thought/believed(?)—it was Mother in heaven watching down over him.

2. As soon as he had his own apartment (in his early twenties), he hung a reproduction of a Lautrec painting of a "tart" on the living room wall. Her face had a pasty, dissipated (deathly) greenish tint. At the same time she seemed to him to be in the posture of Whistler's Mother and reminded him of that good lady. This ambiguous good/bad mother image would "become" Mother sitting in his parlor watching over him, especially when he brought girls home. He and "Mother," depending on circumstances or mood, each could be mostly good, mostly bad, or various permutations and combinations of the two.

3. Still later, while in analysis and at times now observing

himself behaving in ways he could not understand, he "felt" like a puppet on strings, being manipulated by Mother, who was his puppeteer up in the sky.

4. Later in the analysis he spoke of a growing fascination with Italian paintings from the Renaissance period—especially paintings of the Deposition. He was fascinated by the puzzling ambiguity of the contrast between the two Marys—the forgiven Mary Magdalen and the Virgin Mary—grieving together at the feet of the crucified Christ. The problem at this point could be understood as Mother was both good and bad—how to separate and/or fuse and/or reconcile the two.

The sick-dying and then-the-dead mother lay behind the greenish-tinged, bad mother image. I must here supply more history. When Jim was in early adolescence, a neighbor of his, Alfie, who was one or two years older and had been Jim's hero, developed into a "bad boy"—using both soft and hard drugs (pot and heroin), associating with "wild" jazz musicians, and displaying blatant sexual perversions. Alfie was finally hospitalized in a state mental *institution* (diagnosis: schizophrenia), where he committed suicide. The most intense part of Jim's *horror* at all of this focused finally on his fantasy image of Alfie's dead body being cut up by the doctors during the medical examiner's autopsy. He realized that Alfie had been sent to the institution because "something bad was wrong with him." In Jim's most desperately distressed moments—as, for example, after a "sexual failure" or when alone and lonely—the thought would incessantly repeat itself in his mind: "What's wrong with me?" After each premature ejaculation he feared the woman would "send him away"—leave him (which eventually did happen with all but one or two).

This theme was almost instantly woven into his early, developing transference neurosis. At some point during the first six months of analysis, he became involved in a secret daily tryst, consisting of mixed perverse sexual (but noncoital) activities with a psychotic woman who lived in the apartment next to him. (Though he had five sessions a week and knew he was supposed to say whatever came to mind, he didn't tell me about it at the time.) She had pet dogs who defecated in the apartment, and she would clean up the mess with her hands, which she would not wash afterward. She and the apartment smelled of feces and decay. The sexual activities took place at the dining table after she served him food.

While this was occurring but being kept secret from me, Jim reported his first dream: *He was in a doctor's office—Dr. Riker —for an analytic session. Alfie walked in. In horror Jim said, "You are supposed to be dead! Get out of here!" And threw an iron POT at him to chase him out.*

Associations to pot, of course, included drugs and perversion. The name, Riker, he associated to Riker's Island, where juvenile drug offenders were sent at that time—in addition, of course, to Reiser. The dream in free translation said, "Alfie (perversion) stay out of my analysis. If Dr. Reiser learns of my bad thoughts and perversions, he will decide I am crazy and send me to an *institution.*" (Remember the old fear/wish to be sent back to the safety and tranquillity of the *orphanage.*) One aspect of the acting out with the neighbor constituted an escape route from analysis—if discovered, he'd be committed and would escape having to face the "Alfie" in him. One year later—after the neighbor had been committed—he was able (impelled by associations to a later dream and more secure in our relationship) to share the information about his now past behavior with her.

A short time later, there was an interesting encounter and incident which crystallized into a turning point in the analytic work. He started a relationship with an attractive, young professional woman, Sarah, whose mother invited him to have dinner at their home on a Friday evening before he took Sarah out for a date. Jim told me, "She thinks I'm a nice Jewish boy —a good prospect to marry her daughter. If she *knew* what I intend to do later—to take her to my apartment to seduce her! —she'd be shocked and angry." I asked then (using the word "good" as the readily available switch word for the occasion), "What does it mean to be 'good' in bed?" He was ready for it and caught on. "If I am excited and sexy, I'm 'bad'—a bad boy —and I'll lose her. If I'm not potent, I'm bad—a bad lover. If I'm a good lover, I'm a bad boy. I lose her either way, and all the time Mother will be there on the wall watching." It was too late to save the situation with Sarah. He was a good boy and she left—but he understood a lot more.

Much later, early in the last year of his analysis, he had for some time been securely over the premature ejaculation. This had required prolonged working through of sadomasochistic sexual fantasies and castration fears. Remember that he had overheard Father abusing Mother physically before she fell ill and died of diseased sex organs. Shortly you'll understand how that links up psychologically with his separation anxiety.

At this later time he had for almost a year been living with a young woman, Laura, with whom he had a good and mutually deepening loving and respectful relationship. Their commitment to each other had reached the point of planning soon to marry, which they eventually did quite happily and satisfactorily. Their sexual relationship was active and satisfying. There was one annoying problem. Jim felt Laura at times had an offensive body odor. When he finally discussed it with her, she tried a series of deodorant soaps and other such preparations, and used them regularly but to no avail. They realized then that no one else complained (or ever had complained) of the odor. Clearly it was Jim's idiosyncrasy. Around this time Jim found himself fascinated-horrified when he encountered (in reading a novel) accounts of how priests of an ancient civilization would have sexual relations with the bodies of dead young women before embalming them. Memories sprang into his mind of the clutching embraces of his dying mother—in the sickroom that reeked with the stench of the decaying tumor and the putrid discharge that permeated bandages and bedclothes—and yes, of his genital sensations and excitement, AND of his terror, AND of his (child's) loving attraction intermingled with hate and revulsion toward this loving woman— his mother, who had turned into such a horrible and terrifying creature. He realized that his behavior with the psychotic neighbor who smelled; his recurrent fear, "What's wrong with me?"; his wish/fear of being sent away (to an institution); and the memory of Alfie's fate were all connected in his mind.

Laura's body odor, he then understood, was merely the normal smell of healthy female sexual arousal, and it no longer offended him. Our psychological understanding of his sexual difficulties seemed reasonably complete. From the psychoanalytic side, we can surely regard separation-panic as the central core issue, and we can also see how the sexuality of the five-year-old (at the height of the oedipal period) became inextricably entangled and fused and enmeshed in and with it.

The panic states require some discussion, even though it will lead us straight into the dark again. Performance anxiety played a large part in his repetitive episodes of premature ejaculation, and sometimes this anxiety reached near-panic proportion. What about his panic states, in which there was ejaculation without erection and without conscious sexual ideas or impulses? The first attack occurred in his early twenties when he was applying for a job and was given a written test as part of the procedure. During the test he was overtaken by sudden unexpected anxiety that increased to the point of panic, and he had a spontaneous ejaculation. The same thing recurred in similar situations several times after this—when being examined in applying for a job. He developed a phobic avoidance of written examinations, consciously fearing humiliation because he would be visibly wet. Later, spontaneous ejaculation occurred several times in other situations of intense anxiety, for example, being stranded in a small and fragile stalled car at an intersection with the siren and bell of an approaching fire truck getting louder and louder.

For him, applying for a job was in many ways associated with wanting to be adopted. His work history, which began in his late teens, consisted of an endless series of (six-month to two-year) jobs. Each had been in a relatively small laboratory or concern, where he had had a promising start—early "adoptions" by the supervisor or boss, who would act as a mentor. There would be invitations home to dinner, inducing implicit assumptions in Jim that he was becoming "part of the family," a favorite who would eventually be taken in as a "partner." Always it would end in disappointment. Jim would be disappointed in his boss, or his boss would become disappointed with him. He would either quit or be fired—to apply then for the next job.

This was one of the repetitive behaviors of his character neurosis. Remember his childhood experience in the orphanage—his longing to be adopted and his repeated disappointments after being "looked over." I have not gone into his unsatisfying relationship with his father and the series of substitute neighborhood men to whom he had turned as a boy—these also constituted a series of false starts and disappointments. He had an extreme terror of being abandoned, of not being taken in. He could not tolerate being alone. All of these contributed meanings to the process of being examined for a job and made it a particularly charged one that could culminate in panic. Without knowing these historical facts and appreciating their meaning, one might regard the first attack as "spontaneous" and unexplained. On the psychological side, Jim's childhood fear of rejection because of enuresis provides a link to the *idea* of ejaculation through the *idea* of wetness, but there is nothing in the psychological data to suggest exactly how it might link up physiologically with actual ejaculation.

The Interpretive Dilemma

Other cases of spontaneous ejaculation with panic are described and discussed in the medical and psychiatric literature, and it is a symptom that commonly occurs during opiate withdrawal. There is good reason to think that anxiety and ejaculation may be closely related neurophysiologically. Both panic and sexual excitement may share features of central noradrenergic neurophysiology, and this shared neurophysiologic substrate might provide a basis for spontaneous ejaculation during anxious excitement. Could this also be the case with premature ejaculation? Could it be in part a manifestation of performance anxiety? Here we are—in the dark again.

Jim, Another Clinical Example

Recently Redmond, Kosten, and I (Redmond et al. 1983) reported two patients with spontaneous ejaculation (one is Jim, reported very briefly as Case 2 or Mr. B). I think the dual-track approach, which we used there, is helpful at least in avoiding confusion. In that report, approaching from the biological side, the pharmacology of spontaneous ejaculation during opiate withdrawal was used to elaborate a central noradrenergic model. Although there is strong evidence that points to an important role of central noradrenergic systems we reasoned:

It is unlikely that noradrenergic function alone is responsible for the sex-related effects. Instead, other central sexual arousal pathways may be regulated and affected by noradrenergic systems. These related systems may function somewhat independently, depending on the situation, to produce the separation between the usually pleasurable affective state associated with sex and the dysphoric one usually associated with fear. It is also possible that central noradrenergic systems are activated in both circumstances, but the interpretation of the affect is colored by the expected pleasurable resolution, as suggested by Fenichel: 'It is a familiar fact that in the normal sexual process the excitement tension which precedes the release of tension is itself pleasurable, probably in connection with an anticipation in fantasy of the subsequent end-pleasure' (Fenichel 1937). It has also been noted that in certain contexts and for at least some individuals, fear also can be pleasurable. This would suggest that increased noradrenergic function might be compatible with both fear and pleasurable sexual arousal under some circumstances. . . .

These biological hypotheses and speculations allow for the possibility that individual differences in sexual fantasies and their mental associations may be related to differences in the way the CNS mechanisms operate (Redmond et al. 1983, p. 1165–66).

While the hypotheses and speculations derived from converging psychological and physiologic analyses of the symptom of spontaneous ejaculation "allow for the possibility that individual differences in sexual fantasies and their mental associations *may be* related to differences in the way the CNS mechanisms operate," they do *not* close the gap; that is, the exact nature of the relationship is not demonstrated. An example such as the one provided by this clinical account may serve to introduce a note of caution. No matter how closely the two approaches may appear to be achieving full convergence, it may not be possible to achieve actual unified understanding. The distinction may seem to be a fine one; but it is, I think, important nonetheless. Speculations extrapolated from one side or the other—or from the two in concert, as will be exemplified in the next chapter—must be taken with the necessary bit of cautious doubt that this limitation imposes.

CHAPTER 15

Toward a Theory

HAVING FOLLOWED a variety of separate disciplinary paths converging on but failing to reach center (essence) of mind and brain-body, it's time to ask if we've gotten anywhere. Surely we've not gotten to a point where it would be possible to construct a satisfactory comprehensive conceptual model of mind and brain-body in health and disease. Yet I think we've come closer than before to visualizing the nature and shape of part of such a model and closer to specifying some modest but heuristically worthwhile details and working hypotheses. That is what this final chapter will be about. Like what has gone before, it will deal with separate but converging ideas, taking each as far as seems reasonable—but allowing wider latitude for speculation than in earlier sections.

One principle implicit in preceding chapters should be repeated and made entirely explicit here. It is that in thinking about etiologic and pathogenic processes, it is well to bear in mind that there are at least the three main phases in the natural history of disease. Each raises questions unique to it and quite probably involves different mediating processes from those of the other two phases.

The first is the preclinical phase, starting with fertilization of the ovum and establishment of the genome and ending with the onset of active disease process. It may vary in length from minutes, hours, days, or weeks to a lifetime. This is the epoch when questions of specificity—of preprogramming—occupy the foreground. What is the nature of the processes that establish the capacity in particular persons to develop particular diseases?

The second phase consists of the process of precipitation of the active pathophysiology and/or psychopathology and structural changes in tissues if they are part of the disease process. What is the nature of the processes that convert a capacity or potential for disease into an active process?

The third is the period of established disease, extending from time of onset until recovery or death, as the case may be. What changes in pathophysiologic and psychopathologic processes occur with time? What processes mediate remissions and exacerbations? And how may psychological reactions to illness manifest themselves in mental and physiologic function?

The following discussion will deal mainly with questions pertaining to the preclinical and precipitation phases. Available background data show differences between "psychosomatic" and "affective and cognitive" disorders, differences with regard to both premorbid personality and pathophysiology. Accordingly, the discussion, depending upon the amount and nature of the background material, will at various points deal separately with these two disease categories.

The main idea that I am proposing can be simply presented as a postulate which states that *specific preprogramming for disease may reside in the circuitry of the brain and be activated by nonspecific stress responses.*

For such an idea to be taken seriously, four questions must be addressed:

1. How might such preprogrammed pathophysiologic circuits come into being?

2. How might they be related to correlated manifestations in the mental sphere?
3. What are the reasons for thinking that CNS circuitry could be altered or affected in such a way as to permit or enable activation of dormant pathogenic circuits and/or connection of active, but fundamentally isolated, pathogenic circuits to peripheral outflow pathways and effector mechanisms?
4. What might be the nature of such a process?

How Might Preprogrammed Pathophysiologic Circuits Develop? The basic designs or "blueprints" for CNS circuits are carried in the genes, but genetic factors do not always act alone; that is, actual expression of some genes does not occur in all individuals endowed with those genes (incomplete penetrance). Intrauterine, neonatal, perinatal, and postnatal influences, by shaping maturation and development throughout ontogeny, participate in determining what the actual, final functional and structural expression (phenotype) of the potentialities programmed in the genetic material (genotype) will be. Of particular interest in this connection are the "critical periods"—specified epochs during development when the shaping effects of environmental and experiential influences may be maximal. Usually these influences act mainly, often only, within specific time frames. We can cite many examples of environmental agents or forces that exert their effects only during a specific time-limited epoch of development (and are ineffective both before and after that "critical period"): "imprinting" in newly hatched ducklings; effect of rubella virus on fetal cardiac development; in utero effects of some sex hormones on the later behavioral patterns of sexual and aggressive responses displayed by adult animals that have been hormonally exposed during critical periods of fetal life; effects of visual deprivation on development of the structure of (visual) occipital striate cortex (Hubel and Wiesel 1977); effects of absence of or inadequate mothering in infancy on adult social and sexual behavior of monkeys (Harlow 1958). The list could go on and on. Without appropriate stimulation, certain structures and behaviors do not develop; under the influence of excessive or inappropriate stimulation, atypical structural or behavioral effects ensue, some of which become manifest only in later epochs of the life cycle.

Bear in mind that it is the strength and effectiveness of synaptic connections in the nervous system that are affected by learning and experience; that progressive functional development and activation of synapses and circuits in the nervous system proceeds throughout infancy, childhood, and adolescence; and that homeostatic mechanisms probably develop sequentially over time, with certain phase-appropriate homeostatic patterns being especially vulnerable to experiential influence during periods of rapid development or shift; and that these may constitute "critical periods" of exaggerated (or exclusive) vulnerability. Bearing all this in mind, it seems reasonable to think that there are many opportunities for development of brain circuitry to be (adversely) influenced by experience. For example, some patterns of physiologic function change as development proceeds, and patterns appropriate at early phases and ordinarily transient might, under the impact of experience and learning, be rendered more enduring and capable of activation later in life, when they would be inappropriate and even pathogenic. Let me illustrate with a speculative but not illogical example relevant to the circulatory system and of potential interest in connection with (some forms of) essential hypertension.

During a long period of postnatal life, when the infant is still subject to prolonged spells of uninterrupted crying, it would be important (probably necessary) for the infant to have physiologic mechanisms available to produce brisk and sustained increases in vascular peripheral resistance. The reason for this is that each time the infant cries vigorously it exhales against a partially closed glottis, thus increasing intrathoracic pressure and decreasing venous return of blood to the heart. If the crying is sustained, these changes will lead to a fall in stroke volume and cardiac output and result in inadequate perfusion of blood through vital organs. Under such conditions, increase in heart rate and contraction of arterioles would increase cardiac output and raise resistance to blood flow throughout the arterial system, thereby raising arterial blood pressure and ensuring adequate perfusion of heart muscle, brain, and kidneys. Without such a mechanism, or another one to accomplish the same purpose, survival would not seem possible.

Later in development, when prolonged, uninterrupted crying of an infantile type no longer occurs, such a sustained compensatory reflex would no longer be needed—indeed, would be harmful. In the adult, heart rate, peripheral resistance, and arterial blood pressure do rise during increased intrathoracic pressure (Valsalva reflex), but these are quickly and promptly checked by homeostatic reflexes—the carotid sinus and aortic arch baroreceptor reflexes, which increase vagal impulses to heart and arterioles, thus slowing heart rate and relaxing arterioles. To my knowledge, the baroreceptor mechanisms that accomplish this in the mature adult are not yet functionally active in the newborn. They might well not be expected to develop until some later time. Interestingly consistent with such a notion is the fact that patients with essential hypertension demonstrate a circulatory "overshoot" during the Valsalva reflex, evidencing exaggerated blood pressure rise compared to the nonhypertensive adult. Is this overshoot a retained derivative of the infantile response described, retained by the hypertensive patient but not by those with normal blood pressure? An infant with genetically transmitted vascular hyperreactivity would be particularly vulnerable. If such an infant were to undergo severe experiential distress during the appropriate early epoch, might this combination be enough to establish an enduring central "hypertensive" circuit, capable of activation at some future date?

Autonomic functions in the human can be instrumentally conditioned; that is, humans can "learn" to raise or lower heart rate and blood pressure by reward and punishment—biofeedback (Schwartz 1977). Let's speculate further. Suppose an infant with a genetically hyperreactive vascular system was for an extended epoch of early life permitted to cry for prolonged periods before being picked up and comforted (such modes of infant rearing, like some disease vulnerabilities, may "run in families," could even be "related"). Would such repeated experiences—relief at being picked up and held following maximal distress and sustained constriction of the arteriolar bed—somehow shape (by "reward") the hypertensive vascular response and so establish a potentially pathogenic (hypertensive) circuit?

How Might Pathogenic Circuits Be Related to Correlated Manifestations in the Mental Sphere? The best way that I know to address this question was formulated by I. Arthur Mirsky, the investigator who first demonstrated the relationship of the rate of gastric secretion of pepsinogen into blood to the incidence of peptic duodenal ulcer and, indeed, to the capacity to develop the disease. You will recall (chapter 13) that this genetically determined, biological trait correlates significantly with personality traits of patients with duodenal ulcer. Mirsky (1958) hypothesized that this genetically linked, inborn trait would be expressed not only in the physiologic sphere as the capacity to develop peptic duodenal ulcer, but also in the psychological sphere as the constellation of personality traits centering around a core of dependency conflicts that had been earlier described by Franz Alexander. Alexander (1950) had described this constellation as follows:

The central dynamic feature in duodenal peptic ulcers is the frustration of dependent desires originally oral in character. The craving to be fed appears later as a wish to be loved, to be given support, money, and advice. This fixation on early dependent situations of infancy comes in conflict with the adult ego and results in hurt pride, since the infantile craving for help is contrary to the standards of the adult, to his wish for independence and self-assertion. Because of this conflict, the oral craving must be repressed. Oral receptiveness when frustrated often changes into oral aggressiveness, and this also becomes repressed because of guilt feelings it provokes. Both oral dependent and oral aggressive impulses may then be frustrated by internal factors—shame and guilt.

The most common defense against both oral dependent and oral acquisitive impulses is overcompensation. The latently dependent or acquisitive person overtly appears as an independent, hard-working individual who likes responsibility and taking care of others. He responds to challenges with increased activity and ambition, works hard and assumes greater and greater responsibilities. This in turn increased his secret longing to lean on others. . . .

Onset of illness occurs when the intensity of the patient's unsatisfied dependent cravings increases either because of external deprivation or because the patient defends against his cravings by assuming increased responsibilities (pp. 483–84).

Mirsky reasoned as follows. The increased capacity for gastric activity (reflected in higher than normal rate of pepsinogen secretion) would also be expressed behaviorally in the newborn infant as a higher than normal need for satisfaction of "oral" dependency drives. While this assumption, that high rate of pepsinogen secretion would be accompanied by high oral drive and high (oral) dependency behavior, is logical and has face validity, it is not proven. The ideas that follow, then, are speculative.

Mirsky postulated that the mother of an infant with excessive oral dependency needs—even though her nurturant capacity might well be in the normal range—would be unable to satisfy such an infant's demands and so would be experienced as a depriving mother. This would create and progressively amplify reciprocal tensions in the mother-infant relationship—tensions centering on and around satisfaction or dissatisfaction of oral dependent needs. The strain in the relationship would increase as reciprocal frustration and provocation escalated. Core conflicts would cluster around these issues and defenses would be shaped in accordance with them. In adulthood the individual would remember his childhood as a time of deprivation and would manifest the constellation of traits originally described by Alexander as psychologically specific for patients with duodenal ulcer. You will remember that these traits were observed as well in healthy subjects with high rates of pepsinogen secretion—even though they did not have active ulcer disease (chapter 13).

Mirsky postulated, then, that the genetically determined, inborn trait (gastric hypersecretion), through its influence first on the mother-infant relationship and later on other ensuing child-adult relationships, would lead to parallel development of corresponding traits in the psychological realm. These personality traits would correspond to (but neither cause nor result from) the physical expression of the constitutional trait (see figure

15.1). In such a somatic-psycho-somatic model, both psychosomatic and somatopsychic mechanisms (dotted lines) would be regarded as secondary epiphenomena.

Applying Mirsky's conceptual model to the previously cited disease example of essential hypertension, Weiner, Singer, and I (Weiner et al. 1962) postulated vascular hyperreactivity to be the constitutional predisposing, biological trait in that disorder. Hypertension does show a familial incidence, and there are many examples of vascular hyperreactivity in patients with essential hypertension and in prehypertensive individuals as well. Patients with essential hypertension, as mentioned earlier, show an excessive overshoot of blood pressure at the end of the Valsalva reflex. Hypertensive and prehypertensive patients show exaggerated rises in blood pressure to physical stimuli (for example, cold pain, postural change). They show similar rises during some emotionally stressful interviews in the laboratory, but not during those in which they

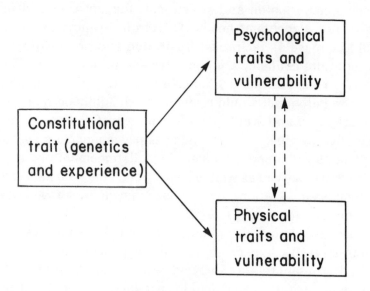

FIGURE 15.1

Developmental Relationship of Psychological and Physical Traits to a Common Constitutional Trait

can control the emotional interchanges through use of highly characteristic "interpersonal insulating" defenses (Weiner et al. 1962).

This last finding led us to speculate in parallel with Mirsky's model that individuals endowed with a hypertensive pressor mechanism may from early infancy on develop specific psychological traits—ego defenses, coping styles, and styles of relating in interpersonal relationships that protect against continuous close and vigorous emotional give-and-take in interaction with others. Interactions in the usual range of intensity might in them evoke vascular overreactions. In fact, patients with hypertension *were* regularly observed to maintain very carefully modulated relationships with others, and it was most often when these insulating defenses broke down that clinical activation of the disease or its aggravation was observed to have occurred. We were able to demonstrate and characterize these defenses in studies both by use of projective psychological tests and by experimental psychophysiologic procedures. And we were able to demonstrate that the psychological and psychophysiologic patterns of response of hypertensive patients to standardized laboratory stimuli differed from the responses to the same standardized stimuli of healthy young adults and a comparison group of patients with peptic duodenal ulcer (Weiner et al. 1962; Thaler et al. 1957).

Patients with essential hypertension, then, "resemble" one another psychologically and psychophysiologically in ways that distinguish them from other groups. This led us to *postulate that these characteristic traits developed adaptively, as protection against a physiologically dangerous constitutional trait.* As mentioned earlier, the circuitry subserving this trait is postulated to have been initially transmitted in the genes, and subsequently, experientially shaped into a psychophysiological hazard by experience.

Regarding affective and cognitive disorders, it is well known that patients with some forms of depressive disorders and patients with schizophrenia display characteristic premorbid personality traits. But the relationship of these traits to potential biological risk markers has not yet been well enough studied to warrant speculations patterned on the Mirsky paradigm (such as those advanced for peptic ulcer and forms of essential hypertension).

What are the reasons for thinking that CNS circuitry could be altered or affected in such a way as to permit or enable activation of dormant pathogenic circuits and/or connection of active, but functionally isolated, pathogenic circuits to peripheral outflow pathways and effector mechanisms? The answer to this question lies in the idea that both the mental apparatus and the brain may operate in multiple modes and that in each sphere output from several circuit modules may compete for a relatively limited number of output channels. In the mental sphere the data of free association led Freud to one of his major discoveries: that the mind simultaneously processes ideas separately and independently in two very different ways, the primary and secondary processes (see chapter 7), and that the person while attending to one mode is consciously unaware of the operations of the other and does not recognize its "printout." Primary and secondary process output compete in complex ways for access to output channels—to consciousness and to motor systems. (In the dream state, when primary process output appears in dream consciousness, the dreaming sleeper lies motionless even though he "moves" in the dream; whatever neural impulses might be intended for the voluntary muscles do not under normal dream state circumstances get through, except perhaps in minuscule quantities—detectable only by sensitive electromyographic recording instruments and mini-movements.) And further, the person in waking consciousness remembers only a small amount of what was experienced in dream consciousness and regards it as strange and for the most part unintelligible.

In parallel fashion, multiple brain circuits could be postulated to be simultaneously active but with limited access to final common effector output pathways. For example, for the simplest case possible one could postulate two competing circuit outputs (A and B), each of which could influence heart rate via the vagal nerve, but the vagus could carry the signals from only one at a time. Circuit A would be generating impulses increasing delivery of vagal tonic, slowing signals to the cardiac pacemaker. Circuit B would generate impulses decreasing the delivery of heart-slowing signals, and so effect an accelerating influence. Depending on which gained access to the vagal fibers, heart rate (assuming other factors affecting it remained constant) would be slower when circuit A was "calling the signals" than when B was, but a switch from A to B would result in an increased heart rate. Or, circuit A could be active and B "dormant"; if B were then to be activated and take over the vagal pathway, the result again would be a change in heart rate—in this example, again an increase. Of course, I am thinking of a much more complicated situation with multiple sets of complex circuit-output modules. For this, permit me to switch metaphors.

Picture, if you will, a TV studio with a live drama in performance. There may be several (four to six or seven or more) cameras recording the scene, each from a different distance, perspective, and angle. Each of the cameras simultaneously and independently feeds into its own monitor screen, which shows the scene according to its input. The director, scanning the monitors, chooses which of the multiple versions he will broadcast to the viewing audience: all circuits are operating simultaneously, only one can be transmitted. Of course, the director can, with dramatic results, switch instantaneously from one to another circuit, or even switch on and use a previously "silent" additional camera that has been in place. Such an arrangement is what I hypothesize in principle for the brain: multiple circuits (some healthy, some pathogenic) arranged in sets that operate simultaneously—but with only one circuit (of a set) at a time having access to a particular "final common pathway" (of neural, neuroendocrine, and neuroimmune mechanisms) that innervates and influences a particular body system, organ, class of tissue or cells, enzymes, and so forth. Although only one circuit at a time can have access to the outflow path connected with its set, the system allows for switching from one to another.

In proposing this hypothesized scheme it is my aim to provide an approximate modeling for one organizational principle (of the many) involved in brain function. The scheme is consistent with a number of important clinical phenomena:

1. Abrupt onset of "night terrors," described by Broughton (1968, 1970) and Fisher et al. (1970). The sleeper in stage 4, the deepest (and a nondreaming) stage of the sleep cycle, suddenly cries out in terror. Heart and respiratory rate increase within seconds (heart rate may more than double and respiration similarly increases or becomes irregular). The facial expression displays terror, matching the person's subjective experience. This is followed by arousal, sometimes by hallucinations and unresponsiveness. The episode, usually of short duration, ends as abruptly as it began and can be interrupted by fully awakening the individual.

2. The characteristic abruptness of both onset and cessation of epileptic seizures of all types—grand mal, petit mal, and temporal lobe attacks.

3. The rapid, dramatic changes in state of consciousness associated with induction and termination of hypnotic states.

4. Rapid, regular switching (at twelve-to twenty-four-hour intervals in some patients) between manic and depressive phases of manic-depressive psychoses.

5. Abrupt and sudden onset of episodes of narcolepsy and cataplexy.

6. Disappearance of striatal rhythmic tremors and rigidity of Parkinsonism and of choreoathetotic movements of tardive dyskinesia during sleep—and their reappearance with awakening.

7. Death following abrupt "turning to the wall" in concentration camp and "death march" prisoners—also in victims of "bone pointing" in primitive societies (Cannon 1923).

8. Rapidly developing psychotic behavior in mass group phenomena (for example, lynchings).

9. Sudden, abrupt onset and cessation of fugues and hysterical dissociative states (remember Carol's, chapter 4).

10. Abrupt changes of personality in patients with multiple personality.

11. Rapid appearance and disappearance of vivid fantasies and psychophysiologic changes (such as vascular headaches) that sometimes occur during psychoanalytic sessions.

12. Abrupt change in range and regulatory patterns of homeostatically controlled autonomic functions (heart rate, respiratory rate, blood pressure, rate of gastric acid secretion, galvanic skin response) with onset and cessation of REM (dreaming) sleep every ninety minutes during a night's sleep. There is clinical evidence

that certain medical accidents—for example, myocardial infarction, onset of hemorrhage from duodenal ulcer, onset of status asthmaticus—may tend to occur more frequently during sleep than during wakeful periods. During REM sleep all autonomically controlled functions show less precise homeostatic regulation, with ranges of activity widened; the physiology is reminiscent of infantile physiology.

Throughout these examples, the words "sudden," "rapid," and "abrupt" are repeated over and over again—the nature of the phenomena force it. This emphatically underlines the idea of abrupt changes in strength, in patterns, and in distribution of stimuli emanating from the central nervous system. The changes effected are not only gross in extent and force but involve abrupt onset and cessation of major organized patterns of social behavior, autonomic function, organized movements (voluntary and involuntary), affect, subjective experience, visceral function, consciousness, memory, mental imagery, thoughts, and even the will to live. These examples are not subtle or esoteric and most are quite common. The nervous system, I think, gives ample evidence that it is quite capable of switching its "circuitry" (or something very much like it) and that it in fact does so with high frequency: regularly as part of healthy living (as manifest in the normal REM cycle and other biorhythms), and quite commonly in response to (mostly unknown) pathogenic vectors.

What might be the nature of a process whereby psychological stress could induce changes in CNS circuitry conducive to or permissive of activation of hypothesized dormant pathogenic circuits and/or connection of active (but functionally isolated) pathogenic circuits to outflow pathways and effector mechanisms? Although, as I think you'll agree, all of the questions in this series of four are rather "heavily armored," this last question is the most impenetrable of the lot. Its unanswerable core, of course, lies in the question of how nonphysical stimuli (meanings) can be transduced into physical physiologic events in the brain (body), a problem that has arisen repeatedly throughout this volume. I've talked (written) all around it, especially in chapters 12 and 13. I can't add anything new here, only summarize and reemphasize some points. What I've post-ulated is essentially the following: The final steps of the trans-duction are probably effected by complex multiple circuits in the hypothalamus. They occur there under the impact of a heavy "barrage" of neural and neurohumoral and chemical stimuli (hormones, neurohormones, neurotransmitters of all types and molecules that modulate and otherwise influence transmission across the synaptic cleft). This barrage, in turn, had its ultimate origin in the highest cortical centers, where meanings are processed (with many of the same neural, neurohumoral, and chemical substances involved), and then traversed the limbic and brain stem structures that are in-volved in affective and affectively influenced associative mem-ory processes.

Regardless of the foregoing verbal barrage (perhaps I should apologize for it), *note that when the stressor is psychological/ psychosocial the entire sequential process starts with meaning and affect, and note that subjective aspects of the experience provide the only window into the intrapsychic essence of the process, and, finally, note also that the psychoanalytic method is the most effective tool now available for penetrating the shadows on the other side of that window.* Unfortunately, data from the psychoanalytic method cannot be meaningfully linked directly to data from biological methods of studying the physi-ologic motor or effector aspects of the stress response.

Meaning . . . . . . Transduction . . . . . . Body response
(Psychology)   (Biology)

Therein lies the challenge and the logical pitfall and, I might add, the heuristic value of a dual-track approach, which ac-knowledges that meanings do not explain physiology and like-wise that physiology does not explain meanings.

In the case of "psychosomatic" diseases, for which patho-genic circuits are postulated in this scheme, I can imagine that the alterations in brain state (biochemical, neurophysiologic, cell biological) could in some way activate a circuit by raising or lowering a threshold and/or connect or disconnect a circuit by whatever means (unknown to me) this is effected under other physiologic and pathologic circumstances (I am referring here to the examples of circuit switching mentioned on pp. 208–9). In the case of affective and cognitive disorders, as already mentioned, the vulnerable central circuitry *is* the problem, so to speak; the vulnerability or risk lies in the very center of the reverberating stress circuitry. It seems somewhat easier for me to imagine how stress mechanisms could set affective disorders off. There would seem to be at least one less step involved; the vulnerable or potentially disordered circuits would not have to be connected to anything else but merely induced into an altered mode of function.

Let me hasten to add that all of the postulates I've advanced concerning precipitation are meant to pertain to its initial phases only (evaluation of meaning, activation of the physiologic stress response and its effect on brain circuitry and output). Surely a lengthy sequence of changes, involving additional factors not discussed, must occur during the process of developing active disease and structural changes in tissues. Such factors would include intrinsic properties of various body tissues, local peripheral metabolic processes and conditions, and additional vectors acting locally and directly on organs and in tissues. The initial steps I have been postulating would in the instance of "psychosomatic" organ pathology lead to preparatory changes in tissues. The importance of these preparatory changes would lie in the postulate that they constitute specific necessary preconditions for the subsequent processes involved in the final actualizing of disease to occur.

The idea that specific preprogramming for disease may (1) reside in the circuitry of the brain (programmed by combined genetic and developmental experiential factors) and (2) be activated by nonspecific stress responses (through their effects of brain circuitry and cell function) carries many implications for empirical research, some of which have been reviewed or alluded to in preceding chapters. It would be beyond the scope of this book to do more than mention a few approaches in broadest outline. I will mention just three. One, already included, has been the method of prospective study of individu-

BODY

als not yet sick known to be vulnerable or predisposed to specific diseases by virtue of possessing known biological markers such as high serum pepsinogen. A second approach consists of prospective and developmental psychophysiologic studies in animal model systems. These allow for systematic programmatic and controlled experimental manipulation of the myriad critical variables and parameters that must be taken into account. For example, genetic endowment can be manipulated by selective inbreeding, parameters affecting maturation of homeostatic systems can be studied in detail (see, for example, Hofer 1981); and learning and social experience can be varied. Relatively simple vertebrates such as rats and mice reproduce rapidly and mature quickly, permitting adequate composition, variation, and matching of experimental groups. Third, modern psychophysiologic techniques should permit empirical investigations into the notion of switching or altering brain circuitry under conditions of altered brain state that have been induced by experimental stress in animals or that might be encountered as "experiments of nature" in the course of clinical work.

I'm led to one last, highly speculative line of thought. Almost everyone was surprised and puzzled when it was discovered that the brain contains a number of peptides (e.g., cholecystokinin, gastrin, vasoactive intestinal peptide) that had long been known to be present in various peripheral body tissues and to have locally appropriate functions. The ones mentioned here were considered to "belong" in the gastrointestinal track— what could they be doing in the brain? Gradually we are beginning to learn that some are widely distributed in brain and function as agonists for some membrane receptors and as modulators of synaptic transmission—some even with behavioral effects! For example, cholecystokinin, which acts as an enzyme involved in digestive functions of the upper gastrointestinal track, has recently been implicated as participating in cerebral regulation of appetite. (The body tissue in which it exists in highest concentration is the cerebral cortex! Coincidence?) Another peptide, angiotensin, long known to originate peripherally in kidney renin systems and to play a role in

212

systemic blood pressure regulation and to be involved in pathogenesis of essential hypertension, also is found in significant
amounts in brain, where it is independently produced. And the
cerebral angiotensin system is involved in regulating systemic
blood pressure but not through the general (peripheral) angiotensin system. What can be made of that?

Ever since I first began to think of peripherally targeted pathogenic central nervous system circuits (more than fifteen years
ago), I've wondered about the possibility that—if they did in
fact exist—they might relate to peripheral predisposing counterparts located in corresponding vulnerable organs or organ
systems. Wouldn't it be exciting if, for example, it were to turn
out that systemic and brain angiotensin systems functioned in
synchrony, that is, "talked to each other," as it were, and did
so in significant ways? Or if stomach gastrin functioned in
synchrony with central cortical gastrin? And so on. It's fun to
think about.

We've become accustomed to stranger ideas than that. After
all, every cell in the body is derived from a single one—the
fertilized ovum—and each cell in the body is endowed with a
complete set of genes, so that originally (before differentiation)
it had the potential to do what any and every other cell in the
body does. During differentiation, genes that will not be used
by the mature cell are inactivated or turned off, leaving "active" only those that will be involved in the special function of
the organ or tissue that the cell will be part of (brain, liver,
kidney, stomach, and so forth). Could this process somehow
allow for functional "dialogue" between "gene related" brain
and peripheral organ functions?

This is a fascinating time indeed in the life and health
sciences, and there is much work yet to be done. The questions
we started with in chapter 1 are all still alive and well—living
in laboratories and clinics everywhere . . . and in our minds.

REFERENCES

Ader, R. (1981) *Psychoneuroimmunology.* New York: Academic Press.

Aghajanian, G. K. (1982) Central noradrenergic neurons: A locus for the functional interplay between alpha-2 adrenoceptors and opiate receptors. *Journal of Clinical Psychiatry* 46:20–24.

Alexander, F. (1950) *Psychosomatic Medicine.* New York: Norton.

Alexander, F.; French, T. M.; and Pollock, G. H. (1968) *Psychosomatic Specificity.* Chicago: University of Chicago Press.

Arnsten, A. F. T., and Goldman-Rakic, P. S. (In press) Selective prefrontal cortical projections to the region of the locus coeruleus and raphe nuclei in the Rhesus monkey. *Brain Research.*

Aston-Jones, G.; Foote, F. L.; and Bloom, F. E. (1984) Anatomy and physiology of locus coeruleus neurons: Functional implications. In *Norepinephrine: Clinical Aspects,* ed. M. G. Ziegler and C. R. Lake. Baltimore: Williams & Wilkins.

Bailey, C. H., and Chen, M. (1983) The morphological basis of long term habituation and sensitization in Aplysia. *Science* 22:91–93.

Balter, L.; Lothane, Z.; and Spencer, J. (1980) On the analyzing instrument. *Psychoanalytic Quarterly* 49:474–504.

Bernard, C. (1864) *Introduction to the Study of Experimental Medicine,* trans. Henry Copley Greene. Ann Arbor, Mich.: Edwards Brothers, 1940.

Bertalanffy, L. von (1964) The mind-body problem. *Psychosomatic Medicine.* 26:29–45.

Brenner, C. (1955) *An Elementary Textbook of Psychoanalysis.* New York: International Universities Press.

Broughton, R. J. (1968) Sleep disorders: Disorders of arousal. *Science* 159:1070–1078.

———. (1970) The incubus attack. *International Psychiatry Clinics* 7:188–92.

Brozoski, T.; Brown, R. M.; Rosvold, H. E.; & Goldman, P. S. (1979) Cognitive deficit caused by depletion of dopamine in prefrontal cortex of rheusus monkey. *Science* 205:929–31.

Cannon, W. B. (1915) *Bodily Changes in Pain, Fear, and Rage.* New York: Appleton.

———. (1923) *Bodily Changes in Pain, Hunger, Fear, and Rage.* New York: Appleton.

Cedarbaum, J. M., and Aghajanian, G. K. (1976) Noradrenergic neurons of the locus coeruleus: Inhibition by epinephrine and activation by the alpha-agonist piperoxane. *Brain Research.* 12:413–19.

———. (1978) Activation of locus coeruleus neurons by peripheral stimuli: Modulation by a collateral inhibitory mechanism. *Life Sciences,* 23:1383–92.

Dahl, H.; Teller, V.; Moss, D.; and Trujillo, M. (1978) Countertransference examples of syntactic expression of warded-off contents. *Psychoanalytic Quarterly* 47:339–63.

References

Darwin, C. (1873) *The Expression of the Emotions in Man and Animals.* New York: Appleton.

Davis, M. (1980) Neurochemical modulation of sensory-motor reactivity: Acoustic and tactile startle reflexes. *Neuroscience and Biobehavioral Reviews.* 4:241–63.

———. (In press) The mammalian startle response. In *Neural Basis of Startle Behavior*, ed. R. Eaton. New York: Plenum Publishing Corp.

Davis, M.; Astrachan, D. I.; and Kass, E. (1980) Excitatory and inhibitory effects of serotonin and sensorimotor reactivity measured with acoustic startle. *Science* 209:521–23.

Edelson, M. (1983) Is testing psychoanalytic hypotheses in the psychoanalytic situation really impossible? *Psychoanalytic Study of the Child* 38:61–109.

Edelson, M. (1984) *Hypothesis and Evidence in Psychoanalysis.* Chicago: University of Chicago Press.

Einstein, A. (1938) Cited in *The Dancing Wu Li Masters* by G. Zukav. p. 8. New York: Bantam Books, 1980.

Engel, G. L. (1977) The need for a new medical model: A challenge to biomedicine. *Science* 196:129–36.

Fenichel, O. (1937) Der begriff "trauma" in der heutigin psychoanalytischen neurosenlehre. Internationale Zeitschrift für Psychoanalyse 23:339–59.

Fisher, C.; Byrne, J.; Edwards, A.; and Kahn, E. (1970) A psychophysiological study of nightmares. *Journal of the American Psychoanalytic Association.* 18:747–82.

Foote, F. L.; Aston-Jones, G.; and Bloom, F. E. (1980) Impulse activity of locus coeruleus neurons in awake rats and monkeys as a function of sensory stimulation and arousal. *Proceedings of the National Academy of Science.* 77:3033–37.

Freud, A. (1946) *The Ego and Mechanisms of Defense.* New York: International Universities Press.

Freud, S. (1895) Project for a Scientific Psychology. In *The Standard Edition of the Complete Psychological Works of Sigmund Freud*, vol. 1. London: Hogarth Press, 1966.

———. (1900) Interpretation of Dreams. In *The Standard Edition of The Complete Psychological Works of Sigmund Freud*, vol. 4. London: Hogarth Press, 1953.

———. (1926) Inhibitions, Symptoms and Anxiety. In *The Standard Edition of the Complete Psychological Works of Sigmund Freud*, vol. 20. London: Hogarth Press, 1959.

——— (1940) An Outline of Psycho-Analysis. In *The Standard Edition of the Complete Psychological Works of Sigmund Freud*, vol. 23. London: Hogarth Press, 1964.

Frisch, K. von (1950) *Bees: Their Vision, Chemical Senses and Language.* Ithaca: Cornell University Press.

Fuxe, K.; Lidbrink, P.; Hökfelt, T.; Bolme, P.; and Goldstein, M. (1974) Effects of piperoxane on sleep and waking in rats: Evidence for increased waking by blocking inhibitory adrenaline receptors in the locus coeruleus. *Acta Physiologica Scandinavica.* 91:566–67.

Gill, M. (1981) *Analysis of transference, vol. 1: Theory and Technique.* Psychological Issues, Monograph 53. New York: International Universities Press.

Gill, M., and Hoffman, I. (1981) *Analysis of Transference, vol. 2: Studies of Seven Audio-Recorded Psychoanalytic Sessions.* Psychological Issues, Monograph 54. New York: International Universities Press.

Gold, M. S.; Redmond, D. E., and Kleber, H. D. (1978) Clonidine blocks acute opiate withdrawal symptoms. *Lancet* 2:599–602.

Goldberger, L., and Breznitz, S., eds. (1982) *Handbook of Stress: Theoretical and Clinical Aspects.* New York: Free Press.

Goldman, P. S., and Rakic, P. T. (1979) Impact of the outside world upon the developing primate brain. *Bulletin of the Menninger Clinic* 43:20–28.

Goldman-Rakic, P. S.; Isseroff, A.; Schwartz, M. L.; and Bugbee, N. M. (1983) Neurobiology of cognitive development. In *Handbook of Child Psychology: Biology and Infant Development*, ed. P. Mussen. New York: Wiley.

216

References

Harlow, H. (1958) The nature of love. *American Psychologist.* 13:673–85.

Hartmann, H. (1958) *Ego Psychology and the Problem of Adaptation.* New York: International Universities Press.

Hofer, M. A. (1981) Toward a developmental basis for disease predisposition: The effects of early maternal separation on brain, behavior, and cardiovascular system. In *Brain, Behavior, and Bodily Disease,* ed. H. Weiner, M. A. Hofer, and A. Stunkard. New York: Raven Press.

Hubel, D. H., and Wiesel, T. N. (1977) Functional architecture of Macaque monkey visual cortex. *Proceedings of the Royal Society of London* 198:1–59.

James, W. (1893) *The Principles of Psychology,* vols. 1 & 2. New York: Holt.

Kandel, E. R. (1978) *A Cell Biological Approach to Learning.* Bethesda, Maryland: Society for Neuroscience.

———. (1979) Psychotherapy and the single synapse: The impact of psychiatric thought on neurobiologic research. *New England Journal of Medicine* 301:1028–37.

———. (1983) From metapsychology to molecular biology: Explorations into the nature of anxiety. *American Journal of Psychiatry* 140:1277–93.

Kandel, E. R., and Schwartz, J. H. (1982) Molecular biology of an elementary form of learning: Modulation of transmitter release by cyclic AMP. *Science* 218:433–43.

Klein, D. F. (1981) Anxiety reconceptualized. In *Anxiety: New Research and Changing Concepts,* ed. D. F. Klein and J. Rabin. New York: Raven Press.

Klein, G. (1976) *Psychoanalytic Theory: An Exploration of Essentials.* New York: International Universities Press.

Klein, M., and Kandel, E. R. (1980) Mechanisms of calcium current modulation underlying presynaptic facilitation and behavioral sensitization of *Aplysia. Proceedings of the National Academy of Science,* 77:6912–16.

Kojima, S., and Goldman-Rakic, P.S. (1984) Functional analysis of spatially discriminative neurons in prefrontal cortex of Rhesus monkey. *Brain Research* 291:229–240.

Kubie, L. S. (1952) Problems and techniques of psychoanalytic validation and progress. In *Psychoanalysis as Science,* ed. E. Pumpian-Mindlin. Standford, Calif.: Stanford University Press.

Leigh, H., and Reiser, M. F. (1980) *The Patient: Biological, Psychological, and Social Dimensions of Medical Practice.* New York: Plenum Press.

———. (1982) A general systems taxonomy for psychological defense mechanisms. *Journal of Psychosomatic Research* 26:77–81.

Lorenz, K. (1965) *Evolution and Modification of Behavior.* Chicago: University of Chicago Press.

Lown, B.; DeSilva, R. A.; Reich, P.; and Murawski, R. (1980) Psychophysiologic factors in sudden cardiac death. *American Journal of Psychiatry* 137:1325–35.

Luborsky, L. (1973) Forgetting and remembering (momentary forgetting) during psychotherapy. In *Psychoanalytic Research,* ed. M. Mayman. Psychological Issues, Monograph 30. New York: International Universities Press.

———. (1976) Helping alliances in psychotherapy: The groundwork for a study of their relationship to its outcome. In *Successful Psychotherapy,* ed. J. L. Claghorn. New York: Brunner/Mazel.

Mahler, M.; Pine, F.; and Bergman, A. (1975) *The Psychological Birth of the Infant.* New York: Basic Books.

Malcove, I. (1975) The analytic situation: Toward a view of the supervisory experience. *Journal of the Philadelphia Association of Psychoanalysis* 2:1–19.

Meissner, W. W. (1980) Theories of Personality and Psychopathology: Classical Psychoanalysis. In *Comprehensive Textbook of Psychiatry* III, vol. 1, ed. A. M. Freedman; H. I. Kaplan; and B. Sadock. Baltimore: Williams & Wilkins.

Miller, J. G. (1978) *The Living System.* New York: McGraw-Hill.

217

Mirsky, I. A. (1958) Physiologic, psychologic and social determinants in the etiology of duodenal ulcer. *American Journal of Digestive Diseases* 3:285–314.

Mishkin, M. (1982) A memory system in the monkey. *Philosophical Transactions of the Royal Society of London* B298:85–95.

⟶ Palombo, S. (1978) *Dreaming and Memory: A new information processing model.* New York: Basic Books.

Pavlov, J. P. (1927) *Conditioned Reflexes: An Investigation of the Physiological Activity of the Cerebral Cortex.* London: Oxford University Press.

Pepper, C., and Henderson, G. (1980) Opiates and opioid peptides hyperpolarize locus coeruleus neurons in vitro. *Science* 209:394–96.

Piaget, J. (1954) *The Construction of Reality in the Child.* New York: Norton.

Redmond, D. E., Jr. (1977) Alterations in the function of the nucleus locus coeruleus: A possible model for studies of anxiety. In *Animal Models in Psychiatry and Neurology,* ed. E. Usdin and J. Hanin. New York: Pergamon Press.

———. (1979) New and old evidence for the involvement of a brain norepinephrine system in anxiety. In *The Phenomenology and Treatment of Anxiety,* ed. W. E. Fann, A. Pokorney, and A. Karacen. New York: Spectrum.

———. (1982) Does clonidine alter anxiety in humans? *Trends in Pharmacological Sciences* 3:477–80.

Redmond, D. E., Jr., and Huang, Y. H. (1979) New evidence for a locus coeruleus—norepinephrine connection with anxiety. *Life Sciences* 25:2149–62.

Redmond, D. E., Jr.; Kosten, T. R.; and Reiser, M. F. (1983) Spontaneous ejaculation associated with anxiety: Psychophysiological considerations. *American Journal of Psychiatry* 140:1163–66.

Reiser, M. F. (1975) Changing theoretical concepts in psychosomatic medicine. In *American Handbook of Psychiatry,* vol. 4 (2d ed.), ed. M. F. Reiser. New York: Basic Books.

———. (1980) Implications of a biopsychosocial model for research in psychiatry. *Psychosomatic Medicine* 42:141–51.

Romanes, G. J. (1883) *Animal Intelligence.* New York: Appleton.

———. (1888) *Mental Evolution in Man: Origin of Human Faculty.* London: Paul.

Rose, S. (1978) Commentary on "Sensory Cortex and the Mind-Brain Problem" by R. Puccetti and R. Dykes. *Behavioral and Brain Sciences* 3:363–64.

Sachar, E. J.; Mason, J.; Kolmer, H. S.; and Artiss, K. L. (1963) Psychoendocrine aspects of acute schizophrenic reactions. *Psychosomatic Medicine* 25:510–37.

Schleifer, S. J.; Keller, S. E.; Camerino, M.; Thornton, J. C.; and Stein, M. (1983) Suppression of lyphocyte stimulation following bereavement. *Journal of the American Medical Association,* 250:374–77.

Schwartz, G. E. (1977) Biofeedback and physiological patterning in human emotion and consciousness. In *Biofeedback and Behavior,* ed. J. Beatty and H. Legewie. New York: Plenum Press.

Selye, H. (1946) The general adaptation syndrome and the diseases of adaptation. *Journal of Clinical Endocrinology* 6:117–230.

Snyder, S. H. (1980) Brain peptides as neurotransmitters. *Science* 209:976–83.

Solomon, G, and Amkraut, A. (1981) Psychoneuroendocrinological effects on the immune response. *Annual Review of Microbiology* 35:155–84.

⟶ Spence, D. (1982) *Narrative Truth and Historical Truth.* New York: W. W. Norton.

Spence, D.; Scarborough, H. S.; and Ginsberg, E. (1978) Lexical correlates of cervical cancer. *Social Science and Medicine* 12:141–45.

Spiegler, B. J., and Mishkin, M. (1981) Evidence for the sequential participation of inferior temporal cortex and amygdala in the acquisition of stimulus-reward associations. *Behavioral Brain Research* 3:303–17.

References

Stein, M.; Keller, S. J.; and Schleifer, S. J. (1981) The hypothalamus and the immune response. In *Brain, Behavior, and Bodily Disease,* ed. H. Weiner, M. A. Hofer, and A. Stunkard. New York: Raven Press.

Thaler, M.; Weiner, H.; and Reiser, M. F. (1957) An exploration of the doctor-patient relationship through projective techniques: Their use in psychosomatic illness. *Psychosomatic Medicine* 19:228–39.

Tinbergen, N. (1951) *The Study of Instinct.* Oxford: Clarendon Press.

Vaillant, G. E. (1971) Theoretical hierarchy of adaptive ego mechanisms. *Archives of General Psychiatry* 24:107—18.

Washton, A. M., and Resnick, R. B. (1980) Clonidine for opiate detoxification: Outpatient clinical trials. *American Journal of Psychiatry* 137:1121–22.

Weiner, H. (1972) Some comments on the transduction of experience by the brain: Implications of our understanding of the relationship of mind to body. *Psychosomatic Medicine* 34:355–75.

———. (1977) *Psychobiology and Human Disease.* New York: Elsevier.

Weiner, H.; Singer, M. T.; and Reiser, M. F. (1962) Cardiovascular responses and their psychological correlates, 1: A study in healthy young adults and patients with peptic ulcer and hypertension. *Psychosomatic Medicine* 24:477–98.

Weiner, H.; Thaler, M.; Reiser, M. F.; and Mirsky, I. A. (1957) Etiology of peptic ulcer. *Psychosomatic Medicine* 19:1–10.

Wilson, E. O. (1977) Biology and the social sciences. *Daedalus* 2:127–40.

INDEX

Acetylcholine, 178
Acting out, 191
Activity-dependent enhancement of presynaptic facilitation, 110
Ader, R., 171
Adrenal cortex, 154, 155
Adrenocorticotropic hormone (ACTH), 152, 154–56
Adenylate cyclase, 113n
Affect: in dreams, 66; instincts and, 83; limbic system and, 165; memory and, 114–15, 210; nodal memory network and, 74–75; primary and secondary process thinking and, 83, 84; reexperiencing of, 95; repression and, 85, 86; signal anxiety and, 88, 127
Affective disorders, 4, 178–83, 185, 211; biological risk markers in, 205–6
Aghajanian, G. K., 146–48
Agoraphobia, 182, 184
Aim of instincts, 82–83; modification and deflection of, 91
Alexander, Franz, 174, 176, 177, 202–3
Alpha-2 adrenoceptors, 147–48
Amkraut, A., 171
Amygdala, 116, 117
Anger, hypothalamus and, 16–17
Angiotensin, 212–13
Animal studies, 4, 103; of anxiety, 126, 127; of cognitive functions, 19, 115; of immune system, 171; of learning, 7, 104–5, 106–11; of memory, 116–22; of preprogramming for disease, 212; of startle reflex, 111–12; of stress response, 141
Anorexia nervosa, 184–85
Anterior pituitary hormones, 152
Anterior tempero-insular region, 116
Anxiety, 6, 86–87; animal studies of, 110, 126, 127; conceptual models of, 14; drugs which reduce, 112; ejaculation and, 187, 193, 194; historical theories of, 125–26; presynaptic facilitation in, 110–11; psychoanalytic theory of, 87; *see also* Signal anxiety; Stress
Anxiety states: chronic, 182, 184; severe, 178
Aplysia (marine snail), studies of, 19, 20, 104, 106–11, 114, 122, 127, 139
Appetite, cerebral regulation of, 212
Arnsten, A. F. T., 152n
Arrhythmias, 170
Arthritis, rheumatoid, 174, 177
Association, 117; *see also* Free association
Association cortex, *see* Prefrontal association cortex
Associative learning, 107, 112
Aston-Jones, G., 150
Autonomic functions: instrumental conditioning of, 201; during REM sleep, 208–9
Autonomic nervous system, 9, 153, 156
Aversion, references to, 40, 43, 60, 61
Aversive conditioned response, 19, 20
Axons, 107

Index

Cortico-limbic-thalamic pathway, 116, 117
Cortico-striatal system, 117
Corticotropin-releasing factor (CRF), 155, 156
Cortisol, 154, 156; immune system and, 171
Countertransference, 22, 79, 95
"Critical periods," 199, 200
Cyclic AMP, 109, 113n

Dahl, H., 49
Darwin, Charles, 125
Davis, Michael, 11–12, 146
Death, fear of, 90
Defenses and defense mechanisms, 33, 36, 82, 91–92, 115; anxiety and, 87; biological roots of, 126; breakdown of, 135–36, 138, 143; in cognitive and affective disorders, 179; development of, 143; of hypertensive patients, 205; immune system and, 171; psychological assessment of, 144; psychosomatic diseases and, 174; unconscious, 34; weakening of, 144
Delayed alternation task, 118–20
Delayed response task, 115, 118, 152n
Dendrites, 107
Dependency conflicts, 202–3
Depression, 178, 180, 182; drugs for treatment of, 149
Desmethylimipramine, 149
Dialectical materialism, 15–16
Diazepam, 112
Dishabituation, 107, 108
Displacement, 65, 66, 68, 75; primary process thinking and, 84
Dissociative states, 208
Diverticulitis, 170
DMI, 120
Dopamine, 112; drug effects on, 123; hypophysiotropic hormones secreted in response to, 156; in prefrontal cortex, 119–20, 122; in schizophrenia, 178
Dreams: in case examples, 43–44, 53–57, 59–63, 94, 191; complex memory systems manifest in, 7; compromise solutions in, 67; Freud on, 64–65; latent content of, 68; nodal memory network and, 72–75; phobic behaviors and, 46–47; physiological-psychological studies of, 6; primary process thinking and, 84, 206; psychoanalytic technique in working with, 69; relation of thoughts to images of, 66, 68
Drives, 82; hypothalamus and, 153; oral, 203; primary and secondary process thinking and, 83, 84; upsurge of, in adolescence and menopause, 144
Drug effects: animal studies of, 112; in cognitive and affective disorders, 178, 180, 182; see also specific drugs
Duodenal ulcer, see Peptic duodenal ulcer

Edelson, M., 5, 99
Ego, 82; signal anxiety and, 90
Einstein, Albert, 14
Ejaculation: premature, 187, 190, 192, 193; spontaneous, 187, 193–95
Emotions: frontal-limbic-hypothalamic pathways and, 153; meaning and, 126; see also Affects
Endocrine system, 152–56, 165; biorhythms and, 172; cognitive and affective disorders and, 178–79; immune system and, 171
Endorphin, 178
Energy, psychic, 84–85
Engel, G. L., 174
"Engrams," 107
Enkephalin (ENK), 147, 149
Entropy, negative, 161
Epileptic seizures, 208
Epinephrine (E), 147
Essential hypertension, 174, 177, 201, 204–6, 213
Evolutionary biology, 125, 145
Experience, effect on synaptic function of, 106, 121, 200

Fantasy: in case examples, 41, 43, 189, 192; memory and, 67; rapid appearance

Index

Index